Praise for *Beyond the Storm*

"Pastor Morton has created an inspirational and instructive guidebook not just for surviving adversity but triumphing over it. Like many who know her, I have been touched and strengthened by her story. *Beyond the Storm* is an indispensable testament to the resilience of spirit, fortified in faith."

—Marc H. Morial, former mayor of New Orleans, Louisiana, and president and CEO of the National Urban League

"Storms are an inevitable part of life. Dr. Debra Morton has courteously and transparently given us a front-row seat to glean from the valuable lessons she learned in, and after, her storms. This is a masterpiece filled with spiritual revelation and practical wisdom on how to navigate through the tumultuous seasons of life and emerge better, stronger, and wiser. To all who are determined not to be a permanent victim but live victoriously beyond the storms of life, this is a must-read. Our trauma can be truly transformational."

—Bishop Joseph Warren Walker III, senior pastor, Mount Zion Baptist Church, Nashville, Tennessee, and international presiding bishop of Full Gospel Baptist Church Fellowship

"A masterful, practical, autobiographical perspective on the essentials of surviving 'storms'—life's threatening encounters. This book is born out of the author's balanced ministry of sitting in the second chair and changing positions to drive the chariot. Beginners in the school of life will find here the secrets of surviving storms. Seasoned students will discover refreshment in the midst of daily pressures. Read and rejoice."

—Ralph Douglas West, founder and senior pastor of the Church Without Walls, Houston, Texas

"Nothing can disrupt our lives like a storm. Whether you are the primary target of its impact, or closely connected to someone who is, we are *never* the same. In the pages ahead, the voice of Pastor Debra Morton calmly coaches and equips us with the necessary tools to clear out the collateral damage and courageously embrace life anew—*beyond the storm*. This is a must-read!"

—Sheryl Brady, pastor of the Potter's House, North Dallas

"God has blessed Pastor Debra Morton with a unique combination of gifts: the fortitude to survive many storms, the awareness of what it took to thrive after the storms, and the ability to teach others the practical application of what she has learned. By sharing her deep understanding in a practical way, she has offered the world tools that can be used to conquer life's most difficult challenges and to convert tragic events into personal triumphs."

—DeForest B. Soaries Jr., senior pastor, First Baptist Church of Lincoln Gardens, Somerset, New Jersey; former Secretary of State of New Jersey; former chairman of the Federal Election Assistance Commission

"Pastor Debra Morton has the courage to bring clarity to our journey through life with Jesus Christ. Storms come to each of our lives at some point and in certain ways. She identifies these different hardships and points the reader to the hope in Christ—trust His Word and learn storm lessons. Hopefully and prayerfully we will read, gain strength, and come through every storm."

—Bishop Jacqueline McCullough, the International Gathering at Beth Rapha, Pomona, New York

BEYOND THE STORM

How to Thrive in Life's Toughest Seasons

DEBRA B. MORTON

NELSON
BOOKS

An Imprint of Thomas Nelson

Published in Nashville, Tennessee, by Nelson Books, an imprint of Thomas Nelson. Nelson Books and Thomas Nelson are registered trademarks of HarperCollins Christian Publishing, Inc.

Thomas Nelson titles may be purchased in bulk for educational, business, fund-raising, or sales promotional use. For information, please e-mail SpecialMarkets@ThomasNelson.com.

Unless otherwise noted, Scripture quotations are taken from the Holy Bible, New International Version®, NIV®. Copyright © 1973, 1978, 1984, 2011 by Biblica, Inc.® Used by permission of Zondervan. All rights reserved worldwide. www.Zondervan.com. The "NIV" and "New International Version" are trademarks registered in the United States Patent and Trademark Office by Biblica, Inc.®

Scripture quotations marked THE MESSAGE are from *The Message*. Copyright © by Eugene H. Peterson 1993, 1994, 1995, 1996, 2000, 2001, 2002. Used by permission of NavPress. All rights reserved. Represented by Tyndale House Publishers, Inc.

Scripture quotations marked NKJV are from the New King James Version®. © 1982 by Thomas Nelson. Used by permission. All rights reserved.

Scripture quotations marked KJV are from the King James Version. Public domain.

Scripture quotations marked ESV are from the ESV® Bible (The Holy Bible, English Standard Version®). Copyright © 2001 by Crossway, a publishing ministry of Good News Publishers. Used by permission. All rights reserved.

Scripture quotations marked NLT are from the Holy Bible, New Living Translation. © 1996, 2004, 2007, 2013, 2015 by Tyndale House Foundation. Used by permission of Tyndale House Publishers, Inc., Carol Stream, Illinois 60188. All rights reserved.

Scripture quotations marked CSB are taken from the Christian Standard Bible. Copyright © 2017 by Holman Bible Publishers. Used by permission. Christian Standard Bible®, and CSB® are federally registered trademarks of Holman Bible Publishers, all rights reserved.

Scripture quotations marked AMPC are taken from the Amplified Bible, Classic Edition (AMPC). Copyright © 1954, 1958, 1962, 1964, 1965, 1987 by The Lockman Foundation.

Scripture quotations marked WEB are from the World English Bible™. Public domain.

Any Internet addresses, phone numbers, or company or product information printed in this book are offered as a resource and are not intended in any way to be or to imply an endorsement by Thomas Nelson, nor does Thomas Nelson vouch for the existence, content, or services of these sites, phone numbers, companies, or products beyond the life of this book.

ISBN 978-1-4002-0833-3 (HC)
ISBN 978-1-4002-0834-0 (eBook)

Library of Congress Control Number: 2018967246

Printed in the United States of America
19 20 21 22 23 LSC 10 9 8 7 6 5 4 3 2 1

It is with great joy that I dedicate this book first to my husband, "Honey" (my hero), and my three lovely children: Jay, PJ, and Xani. I love you very much. Together we have weathered many storms in the public eye. You have been amazing. It is because of your remarkable strength and never-ending support that I was able to write this book that will hopefully help families grow and experience success. Thank you!

Secondly, much love and appreciation to my team, my two church families, Greater St. Stephen and Changing a Generation, and the Full Gospel Baptist Church Fellowship. Each of you are acquainted with my storms because you have been there through most of them. Thanks for your prayers and votes of confidence. You have shaped and sharpened me. Special thanks to Raoul and Ascendant Group Branding for believing in me. Much love to Rainah.

Finally, to the people of my birthplace: NOLA Katrina survivors. It was tragic, but you have taught the world how to weather a storm. The secret (no secret to me) to your resilience is your heart. You always hear a beat and as long as your heart hears the beat you will live, love, and give! Don't ever lose heart and don't just survive—thrive!

Contents

Foreword

Dr. Debra B. Morton, whom I'm so proud to call my wife, has written one of the best books I have ever read. As I reflect on our lives together of more than forty years, I can recall when I met her. She was in college but postponed her pursuit of a degree in communications to become a full-time wife, mother, and commit fully to the role of a pastor's wife. However, she was determined to go back to finish and pursue all that God had put inside of her, and I am so glad that she did. In fact, I'm confident that all who read this book will be glad as well.

Her gift to communicate in a real way with others is un-paralleled, as you will see in this amazing book, *Beyond the Storm*. She skillfully breaks down three areas: Before the Storm, In the Storm, and Beyond the Storm. I can personally relate to all three because we went through these three phases together.

Debra is and has always been very detailed. Her memory is like no one else I know. I wish she would forget some things, but she remembers it all and tells it well. I've learned that this is what is needed if one is going to get beyond the storms of life and flourish. It brought tears to my eyes as I recalled how, together, we faced some of the greatest storms in life.

This is a must-read because everyone can remember "before the storm" when life was great and wonderful, and many can identify with being "in the storm" because they are there right now. Yet, we all can praise God right now, in the midst of the storm, because Debra gives so much practical information and spiritual insight on weathering the storms of life. *Beyond the Storm* is a story that God will use to not only carry you through a storm but empower you to thrive thereafter.

I believe it is essential, for those of you who have been or are presently in a storm, to hear from someone who's been through one and can show you how to get beyond it. Pastor Debra is not only an eloquent and informative writer, but her work is further strengthened by her personal victories in storms. So sit back and enjoy. When you are finished, you will definitely know how to get *beyond the storm.*

I'm so grateful that I'm married to this genius. It would have been next to impossible for me to have made it if it wasn't for her in the storms with me.

Thanks, my love, for this awesome book!

—Bishop Paul S. Morton Sr.,
founder, Full Gospel Baptist Church
pastor, Changing a Generation FGBC, Atlanta
copastor, Greater St. Stephen FGBC, New Orleans

Introduction

The Storm Playbook

I once asked a psych nurse, "What is the difference between someone who loses their mind and goes crazy during a difficult experience and someone who has a similar experience but can go on with their life?"

Her answer was unbelievably simple: "Coping skills."

Those two little words pack a powerful punch. No matter what kind of family you come from, no matter your educational background or your socioeconomic status, if you live in this world long enough, you will eventually face something that will rock your world, a life "storm."

One of the most difficult examples I can think of is losing someone you love. Afterward, friends and family will gather around, bring comforting meals, and offer emotional support. However, soon after the funeral is over, after the casket is lowered into the ground and everyone returns to their lives, you are left alone to pick up the pieces and try to figure out how to walk in your new "normal."

Your personal strategies and selected coping mechanisms all play an enormous role in how you adjust to life after loss, tragedy, or trauma. I know firsthand what it feels like to put the pieces of your life back together after a devastating loss. This book, simply stated, is a playbook to give you an arsenal of coping skills. It is designed to help you process difficult situations and assist you with surviving those challenges by outlining relevant, practical steps you can implement in your daily life to push forward through setbacks and agonizing circumstances. As you begin to use the techniques and strategies illustrated in these chapters, I hope you will be able to come into alignment with God's purpose for your life, renew your hope, reclaim your passion for life, and experience fulfillment and joy. Many books have already been written about life after tragedy, but I want to provide clear-cut strategies for surviving, recovering, and thriving after tragedies, traumas, and trials.

I have discovered, through my experiences, that there is a difference between surviving and thriving. Survival is good, but thriving is better. To survive is to continue to live or exist in spite of danger or hardship. In many cases, though, people exist but don't really live life after extreme situations happen to them. On the other hand, to thrive is to grow or develop well, to prosper or flourish. It is God's desire that we do not merely exist after storms but grow, develop, and flourish in every way! The instructions, strategies, and examples given in this playbook are designed to help you do just that. No matter what kind of challenge you face, *thrive*.

There are many different types of losses and challenges we can experience, but I have learned that afflictions and difficulties ultimately fall into these main categories:

- **Expected**, such as the prolonged illness of a loved one
- **Unexpected**, such as a fatal car accident
- **Avoidable**, such as a tragedy/loss that was preventable (for example, a house fire caused by faulty wiring)
- **Unavoidable**, such as a tragedy or loss that could not be prevented (for example, a parent with a genetic disease)

I emphasize the plurality and diversity of losses and challenges because while it is difficult to recover from one hurt, it can seem impossible to get over two or three facing you all at one time. However, I am a living witness that it is absolutely possible.

I have discovered that one way to ensure that you can adjust appropriately and continue to live an emotionally healthy life through crisis is by learning how to distinguish between helpful and harmful coping strategies and then implementing the helpful ones while avoiding the harmful ones.

As you can see from the list below, there are many types of beneficial coping mechanisms:

- **Adaptive mechanisms:** those that offer definite help
- **Behavioral mechanisms:** those that change what we do
- **Cognitive mechanisms:** those that change what we think
- **Conversion mechanisms:** those that change one thing into another

Psychologists have also identified negative coping strategies that can be a hindrance to healing. These can make the situation worse rather than better:

- **Attack mechanisms:** those that push personal discomfort onto others
- **Avoidance mechanisms:** those that avoid the issue
- **Defense mechanisms:** those you use to defend yourself. There are many of them, but two of the most common are displacement and projection.
- **Self-harm mechanisms:** those that hurt us when we use them

We will discuss these in greater depth in chapters 5 and 7 so that you can be aware of and avoid the negative coping strategies while embracing the positive ones, making them a part of your very own Storm Playbook.

It is crucial for you to learn about these techniques because when life gets rough, it doesn't matter who you are, it hurts. My husband and I are pastors, and we have been very successful in ministry, but when Hurricane Katrina hit us in 2005, it was a tough, challenging, and painful time. That experience, along with several others, has given me some practical keys that I believe will assist you in recovering from whatever life is throwing your way.

How to Use This Book

This book has several sections to assist you in applying the information to your life. First, I want to encourage you to get a small journal or notebook and take notes during your journey. Use this writing time to identify and address the overwhelming situations that are sucking all the joy from your life. I have been there and lived through it, and you can, too, but you must be intentional and take time to process the event that is taking such an emotional, physical, mental, and/or sociological toll on you. You can do that by using this playbook to unlock buried or forgotten truths or issues regarding your storm, including

- identifying the source of your pain;
- creating a clear plan to move forward;
- developing your plan step-by-step; and
- knowing and deciding the parts you must "own" alone, as well as the areas where you may require assistance from others.

Besides being an interactive tool to help you actively assess and overcome your hurts and difficulties, *Beyond the Storm* will help you change how you see the storms in your life. In order to do this effectively, there are Storm Studies at the end of each chapter that include chapter summaries, journaling questions, Scripture studies of storm survivors, and memory verses. Some of the chapters have a few alternate sections, but rest assured, they are all designed to help you make the most out of your time with this book. Although life is hectic and busy, I believe taking the time to complete these activities is well worth it. It will not only help you navigate the effects of your past and prepare for future storms but also teach you how to look beyond your storms so you can actively pursue the purpose you were designed to fulfill.

CHAPTER 1

Life Before
the Storm

Before we venture into the storm, I want to share a little more about me. I'm a native of New Orleans, where I graduated from high school. I had planned to go to UCLA to major in communications; my dad, however, insisted it was too far away. I was agitated at his disapproval, but I conceded and decided to enroll at the University of New Orleans. That fall, when I was about to begin my college classes, my future husband, a young man all the way from Canada, started attending my church. Weeks after joining our church, on a November morning around Thanksgiving, he shared the testimony of what God had done in his life and how he ended up in our city. In a nutshell, he had lost everything and felt as if God was specifically saying, "Get to New Orleans."

Like Jonah in the Bible, this young man was hesitant to follow the leading of the Lord. He thought, *I don't even know anybody in New Orleans.* But he realized that trying to rebel wasn't working. After all, someone had stolen his car with all his clothes and other belongings in it. He stated how extremely painful that was, because he had very little money to replace the things he had lost. He admitted that it shook his faith. So he stopped resisting and said, "Lord, I'm going." He took a Greyhound bus and made his way to New Orleans.

It seemed logical then that after relocating to New Orleans he would start attending the church nearest his new home, which was my church. He decided to become a member there. We know now it was divine destiny.

The older people were impressed with his testimony. All the older ladies were chattering, "He's such a fiery young man." Later, when I got home, even my granny said, "Oh, wasn't that a powerful testimony?" I smiled at her, but I laughed to myself, because I was busy in college and not interested in having a boyfriend.

Time passed, and about a month later, I sang a song at our preservice, where we held discipleship training. I had a huge Afro—keep in mind, it was the seventies—and when the service was over, that same young man came up to me and said, "That was a beautiful song. By the way, the Lord said you're going to be my wife." I was so taken aback that I started avoiding him whenever he was around. But he kept pursuing me, and eventually we became friends and started dating. After two years, he asked me to marry him.

That man, Paul S. Morton, turned out to be a phenomenal husband of forty-one years, a remarkable pastor, a wonderful singer, an exceptional preacher, and an excellent father. From that union, we had three children—two girls and a boy. We have had highs and lows, but all in all, we have created a great life in our many years together. People always ask us our secret to staying together for so long. We say God is the third person in our marriage. He makes the difference.

When we were first married I did not work in ministry, but we have now celebrated more than thirty years serving together, twenty-five of those years as pastor and co-pastor of Greater St. Stephen Full Gospel Baptist Church in its three locations. We are grateful that, while ministry is time consuming, we were able to build and enjoy a wonderful personal life with each other, our children, extended family, and friends. All this was life before the storm, Hurricane Katrina. Amazingly, after the storm we organized a new church, Changing a Generation Full Gospel Baptist Church in Atlanta, Georgia, and have been co-laborers in its growth for twelve years.

A year before Katrina, I also assisted my husband with another church he had planted in Arabi, Louisiana. It, too, was called Changing a Generation. A pastor was installed there but later was led to relocate. At that time, we already had seven weekly services among our three locations. As his co-pastor, I thought eight services would overload my husband, so I felt the need to step up and offer to lead the church in Arabi until another pastor was found. Within months my husband was led to install me as the senior pastor. It was scary and challenging, but also intriguing. Unfortunately, before a year had passed, Katrina hit and the church in Arabi was destroyed. We were saddened but realized as we began to reorganize in Atlanta that God had been preparing us for the new thing He was going to do—operate both independently yet interdependently in ministry. He was preparing and teaching us how to thrive after a storm, not just survive.

While serving at the new church in New Orleans as senior pastor, I was excited that God had blessed me with the surprising opportunity to help sustain and grow it. I was being developed in areas of leadership and decision making as well as being trained to be sensitive to God's voice. At the very start, I was given a word from God to schedule the worship service on Saturday rather than Sunday. I named it "Live at Five." The new church service change was fresh and fun but also wisdom from above, because it allowed me to continue to assist my husband with the other services at Greater St. Stephen.

Wisdom is the application of knowledge. The Bible says in Proverbs 4:7, "Wisdom is the principal thing; therefore get wisdom: and with all thy getting get understanding" (KJV). As I look back, it was definitely the Lord's leading for me to offer to help with the Arabi church; and although we did not rebuild the Arabi church, the experience of working there gave me the additional skill set I would need to help my husband rebuild the other locations in New Orleans and start the new ministry in Atlanta. I was given greater responsibility following Katrina as a co-pastor and in the new position of pastor in Atlanta. Dealing with the smaller challenges in Arabi gave me the ability (with God's help) to handle the larger congregation in New Orleans.

———

I still remember August 2005 like it was yesterday. We had just moved into our dream home, and our churches were thriving. The day before the storm I held my Saturday service in Arabi, Live at Five, right on schedule. One of our members had brought her entire family reunion to it. I stood around afterward exchanging hugs and conversation, but people kept coming up to me asking if I had heard about the storm. After the third person mentioned it, I left the church and decided to pick up some items from the grocery store before the storm hit.

I started to feel more urgency when I walked into the local convenience store and saw there was only one loaf of bread left on the shelf. I quickly grabbed it and headed to the counter, but before I could get out my wallet, the cashier informed me she couldn't sell it to me because she was holding it for the manager. People were becoming fearful, and some were even acting desperate as they got more information about the storm. After going back and forth for a bit, she finally gave in and let me buy the bread. Next, I stopped at a Chinese restaurant, and after I ordered my food, the cook in the kitchen appeared with a big pot of shrimp fried rice and told me I could take it all because they were shutting down for the night. I hurried home immediately. If the restaurant was giving away food, I thought to myself, *This storm must be severe.*

As soon as I walked in the door, my husband started giving me his own live weather report. At this point, I still did not understand the gravity of the storm that was approaching. New Orleans natives had adopted a culture of "riding out the storm" because during the past century, hurricanes had flooded New Orleans five times: in 1915, 1940, 1947, 1965, and 1969.[1] But when I saw the look on my husband's face as he described the forecast, I realized I needed to stop teasing him for always being glued to CNN. In fact, this storm convinced me I need to pay more attention to the news channels.

Although it was clear to me that a hurricane was coming, I wanted to stay in our house on the second floor during the storm. My thinking was that our stucco home was only one year old and strong. I had survived former storms in older one-story wooden homes, so I thought certainly this house could protect us, but my husband had already decided what we would do. I might point out here that all storms aren't the same, which I will discuss later, and therefore each one may require "different movement."

Since the mayor had issued a mandatory evacuation and the airport was shutting down at noon the next day, my husband told me the details of the schedule for services the next morning and said that afterward we would fly out. New Orleans was in trouble because of its unusually high risk for flooding—the average elevation is about six feet below sea level, and the city is surrounded by water. Neighborhoods that sat below sea level, many of which housed New Orleans's poorest and most vulnerable people, were at significant risk of flooding. Officials worried that the surges could overtop some levees and cause short-term flooding, but no one predicted what would happen after Hurricane Katrina, when the levees collapsed. Thank God we left when we did; our home was in one of the areas that was hit the hardest.

Those few days, from Saturday morning through Monday evening, were a complete whirlwind. Saturday evening I immediately began making arrangements for my ailing mother, sister, and aunt, all of whom were my responsibility.

They were in medical facilities and in no condition to fly. I felt helpless. I contacted the facilities and a sitter to make arrangements for their care. Each facility assured me that their evacuation plans were already in progress; they would take them to a sister facility where they would be safe. My mind was racing with the what-ifs; however, at that moment, I had to place my trust in God and those administrators because there was nothing else I could do.

My husband, children—ages eighteen, twenty-four, and twenty-eight—along with my daughter's husband and two kids (a two-year-old and a nine-month-old), and I packed our essentials and went to bed. The next morning, which was Sunday, we got up, preached at our service in New Orleans East, and instructed our assistant pastors at our New Orleans uptown location to urge our church family to obey the mayor and evacuate. The service at our third location, located on the west bank of New Orleans, never happened because it was scheduled for 11:30 a.m., and evacuations were in full effect by then. We also followed the mayor's instructions and boarded a plane, heading east, because we had speaking engagements scheduled for that upcoming week, first in New Jersey and then in Oakland, California. The pilot became ill, though, so he diverted the flight to Memphis, where we slept in a hotel for a short time. When the pilot awakened us, he informed us that the storm was headed toward our exact location, so we evacuated again with our children and grandchildren.

After we finally arrived in New Jersey, our family started to relax, but while my husband was talking to us, he suddenly stopped. I waited for him to continue, and when he finally did, he asked me to call the church where he would be speaking to tell them he would not be coming. He put his head in his hands and whispered a soft prayer. While the children and I attempted to get him to tell us what was wrong, he handed us his phone. He had received a text from a family friend that contained a picture of our tallest, most significant church building in New Orleans East—it was entirely submerged by water except for the very top of the steeple. All our locations were damaged by the storm, but this one was hit the hardest.

We all felt his extreme devastation; however, my perspective was about moving forward. Although he resisted, I encouraged my husband to go ahead and preach. I reminded him and our children that we were no longer in the storm. We had made it out. At first he was not receptive to my point of view at all. He was so gripped with the grief of the devastation he had seen in that photo that he was inconsolable. I understood, but somehow I looked beyond that.

Emotions during devastation and challenges can be hard to control, and we cannot deny them because they are very much a part of being human. There are moments when life allows us to "stay there" a minute, to lock ourselves up in a room alone to weep or scream or curl up in a blanket and stare out the window all day. Been there, done that. On the other hand, there are times we must push past our emotions to keep our sanity and grab hold of our new normal.

I'm reminded of a story about King David, who taught this lesson during a huge storm in his life.

> And it came to pass, when David and his men were come to Ziklag on the third day, that the Amalekites had invaded the south, and Ziklag, and smitten Ziklag, and burned it with fire;
>
> And had taken the women captives, that were therein: they slew not any, either great or small, but carried them away, and went on their way.
>
> So David and his men came to the city, and, behold, it was burned with fire; and their wives, and their sons, and their daughters, were taken captives.
>
> Then David and the people that were with him lifted up their voice and wept, until they had no more power to weep.
>
> And David's two wives were taken captives, Ahinoam the Jezreelitess, and Abigail the wife of Nabal the Carmelite.
>
> And David was greatly distressed; for the people spake of stoning him, because the soul of all the people was grieved, every man for his sons and for his daughters: but David encouraged himself in the LORD his God. (1 Sam. 30:1–6 KJV)

Often when devastation hits we look for external things to soothe or fulfill us, but we must pull strength from within. King

David wept when he saw that what he valued was gone, but he inquired of God through prayer as to what he should do. Scripture says that afterward he encouraged himself. We must learn to pull ourselves out of dark situations by looking to God in order to discover the strength that's beneath the surface— under that hurt, sadness, confusion, and emptiness—and pull out healing for our souls.

So I gave my husband an encouraging push and challenged him to change his perspective, then left him alone at the hotel for a while to regroup. Later, when I returned, we received a call from a CNN reporter who had learned we were nearby. He asked my husband to come and speak on behalf of those who, like us, were victims of the chaos of Katrina. He accepted the invitation and spoke on camera, encouraging the people of Louisiana, his church family, the nation, his natural family, and, most important, himself. People expressed to us how encouraged they were after seeing and hearing him. When he finished speaking, he had found the strength to go on and complete his scheduled assignment—a preaching engagement in New York, which was very close to our hotel in New Jersey. God ministered to him while he was ministering to our churches and the world. Looking at King David again, when he was extremely down and out from the loss of family and possessions, he found enough strength to ask God what he should do next in his storm. David realized his assignment from God to care for humanity was not over. It was time to recover all. I was so heartened by his rekindled courage.

Here, I believe, it is important to speak about devastation and leadership. If you are a leader in a challenging situation, it can be overwhelming, especially when you are hurting as well. However, "whom God calls, He qualifies." Throughout my ministry years,

I have been able to observe many people, from a distance and up close. God gives His leaders additional stamina, insight, confidence, and supernatural faith to move through these situations. When Moses was asked to approach the evil Egyptian king and command him to let the Israelites go, he said to God, "I'm nobody special to represent You. I can't speak on the people's behalf; I'm not articulate, and I have no real power to overtake him" (Ex. 4). Most people who are called to lead never feel adequate or qualified. However, when they answer the call, they do things so amazing that they are amazed themselves.

I have also seen strong leaders emerge during calamity. Just like Moses, these leaders begin to tell God why they are not the ones who should go, only for God to prove they were always the leaders meant for that appointed time. They are like those first responders who come out of nowhere and save people from otherwise fatal situations. The leader in them responded so quickly that they shocked themselves. After the CNN appearance, I watched my husband shift from survival mode to thrive mode.

Although my husband told me that Satan had said "it was over for him," and despite the many people who wrote ugly things on the internet about our loss, the thing my husband held on to was God telling him that his latter days would be greater than his former. For him, Hurricane Katrina was a Category 5 storm. He felt, at his age, it would be hard to rebuild. To add to that, Satan gave him a visual of his loss when someone, trying to be helpful, texted that picture, taken from a helicopter, of our largest church facility underwater. I told him, "Honey! Stop worrying and don't look at that picture. We are still alive and able to go on. God will sustain us." He called me his "aggravating angel." I'll take that.

My husband and I both weathered the storm, but we learned

different lessons from it. My husband's ministry load increased. It seemed like the entire world was looking to him for inspiration and direction during and after the storm, yet he was in the midst of the storm himself. As a true helpmeet, I began to encourage him.

Later we would learn that we had lost most of our material possessions. Our dream home, pictures, clothes, and belongings were all gone, as 80 percent of our beloved New Orleans was flooded with stormwater. The two things I did have, though, were my family and my faith. To this day, that has made all the difference in how I view the storm, and that is my first lesson for you. No matter how bad life looks, when you have your family and your health, when you are still breathing and functioning—or as our elders would say, "still in your right mind"—you have a lot to be grateful for. Because when you've lost something precious, something irreplaceable, the material things that can be replaced become less significant.

Gratitude is everything. Learning how to be grateful for what you have left is sometimes the very key to surviving a tragedy. You have probably heard the adage, "When life gives you lemons, make lemonade," but I am here to tell you that sometimes there is no sugar and you have to find something else to do with the lemons. Sometimes you just have to be determined to see the glass half-full instead of half-empty, and other times you have to be content with just having a glass.

My point is that all the cute sayings and social media quotes are great, but in life when the rains come and the storms howl, you must be determined to live life after the storm. And this book is dedicated to motivating you to do just that. I am so excited that you have decided to take this journey with me.

The Eye of the Storm

Before I dive into the storm lessons, I want to share with you how I was inspired to write this book. After we survive a storm, and life is pretty much back to normal, we see things a little more clearly. We can look back with hindsight that offers a helpful perspective. This type of understanding may feel like it comes out of nowhere, when we least expect it. But this "sight" is why I'm so sure that life is a journey with a beginning, middle, and end.

I am also entirely convinced that there is a Power guiding each of our lives for a purpose. Regardless of what school faculty are required to teach, I do not believe we came out of nowhere. The creation story in Genesis provides evidence to the contrary. The problem with teaching individuals that they evolved over time from cavemen is that it eliminates an important piece of the first man's dilemma. God said that it was not good for Adam to be alone, so He put Adam to sleep and created a suitable helpmeet for him, Eve. The same way that God knew from the beginning of time that Adam should not be alone, I also believe that we need to exist in a world with meaningful human connection from day to day. People have a right to believe whatever they want. But it does make me sad to imagine the fulfillment they are missing because of that disconnected mind-set.

I receive such joy, understanding, and satisfaction from the power of divine connection with mankind (spending time with my family, friends, and congregants) and nature (some of the best and most relaxing times of my life have been spent enjoying beach sand and ocean waves). For me, times of connecting with people and enjoying scenic escapes are indispensable. Our human connections and positive life experiences can calm us when the storms of life begin to pour devastation upon us. Although the difficulties that occur in storms are daunting, I can stand firm because I believe in a divine Power that always will work out every situation for my good as long as my mind-set and actions align with God's will and purpose for my life.

I was inspired to write this book after I had been meditating about my life for months. I knew I was to write a book. As I wondered what the book would be about, my thoughts were interrupted, and I heard, "You're a grown woman now because you weathered the storms." I responded, "Yes, I am!" I became even more excited and grateful as I pondered all the things I had survived.

I was reminded that Hurricanes Betsy, Katrina, Rita, and others were not the only storms I had been through! I had been through many other storms that didn't contain bad weather but bad conditions. I had even survived what I call "baby storms." I realize most grown men and women were once broken little boys and girls because of baby storms. Baby storms are the things we went through before we actually knew how to spell *storm*; we were too young to understand the depth and effect of the hurt, despair, and damage certain situations had on us. Unfortunately, as we grew to adulthood, we then discovered we had scars we couldn't really explain. I believe through this book, if you allow Him, God will perform supernatural plastic surgery on you to remove the scars and stigma of shame, disgrace, hurt, devastation, pain, insecurity, and fear, and you will experience a life that's victorious.

Weeks after I was inspired to write this book, I was in a car riding through the SoHo area in New York with my godbrother, enjoying the weather, when I had a vision. I said to him, "I just got a vision for a painting." I shared it with him, and he said he knew just the artist to make it come alive. In the vision, I saw stormwaters. People were running, crying, and swimming; others were in boats being rescued by first responders. I knew it was a mental picture of that dreadful day of Katrina. The water was tumultuous, and the winds were fierce. Something spoke to me in that vision, saying, "This is when the eye of the storm hit." It saddened me.

The eyewall of the storm is the worst part of any storm. When it hits, it destroys, and when it hit New Orleans, the destruction was mind blowing. Although this vision happened years after the hurricane, I was shaken; that part of the scene still evoked a certain amount of emotion in me. However, the interesting thing about the vision was that there was an actual eye in the midst of the storm, a human eye that was looking at everything. It caught my attention and moved me away from all the chaos.

As I came out of the vision, I understood the revelation of it. God explained to me that the eye above the disaster was His eye. Yes, He saw the storm, and although the eyewall of a storm is the most destructive part, His eye is always there to get our attention and help us realize that if we look to Him, we will not only survive the storm but thrive beyond the storm. Later I realized that vision was God fine-tuning the content for the book I would write.

No, Katrina is not the only storm I've been through, but each time I have experienced one I have walked away with invaluable insight that I am compelled to share. I pray it will help everyone who reads this book connect the dots and paint a brand-new picture after each storm.

Storm Playbook Study

Chapter Summary
- Although it can be challenging to watch the news and keep up with current events, particularly because of the negativity that results from that, it is important to stay in the know about things that can affect your life such as weather forecasts, national product recalls, prominent and local deaths, and so forth.
- Gratitude is essential for living a positive life. Being able to focus on the positive while acknowledging the negative (not being in complete denial of challenge) is crucial.
- During the darkest hours of your life, one way to find encouragement is to become a source of encouragement for someone else.
- Meaningful human connection is not optional. God did not think it was a good idea for Adam to be alone, and the same is true for you and me.

Journaling
1. Gratitude is a major component discussed in this chapter. How can you maintain your "attitude of gratitude" during the challenges you face?
2. My husband gained strength by encouraging others when he was deeply devastated by the storm's effects. Whom can you encourage and strengthen in times of challenge?

Storm Survivor: Joseph
Joseph is a wonderful example of a storm survivor. His storm troubles began brewing early. First, he was his father's favorite,

which created tension and animosity between him and his brothers. Next, his father demonstrated his special love for Joseph by giving him a coat of many colors. The brothers barely contained their simmering envy at the gift, and it soon turned to burning hatred when Joseph shared two dreams that seemed to imply the family would one day bow down to Joseph. The brothers decided to act on this hatred one day when they were out with their father's flocks, planning to kill Joseph but first throwing him into a cistern (Gen. 37:18–24). Then they had a "better" idea:

> As they sat down to eat their meal, they looked up and saw a caravan of Ishmaelites coming from Gilead. Their camels were loaded with spices, balm and myrrh, and they were on their way to take them down to Egypt.
>
> Judah said to his brothers, "What will we gain if we kill our brother and cover up his blood? Come, let's sell him to the Ishmaelites and not lay our hands on him; after all, he is our brother, our own flesh and blood." His brothers agreed.
>
> So when the Midianite merchants came by, his brothers pulled Joseph up out of the cistern and sold him for twenty shekels of silver to the Ishmaelites, who took him to Egypt. (vv. 25–28)

Although the story begins in Genesis 37, it does not end here. You can continue reading about Joseph's defeats and victories in Genesis 39–50.

Joseph's brothers first wanted to kill him, but then they settled for selling him into slavery. But, as you follow the life of Joseph, you find that he maintained a positive outlook, held fast to his integrity, and left every place he landed in better condition than it was before his arrival. Joseph's story is a pivotal example to all of us that even when storms come into our lives that lead us into negative situations and unfortunate circumstances, God is always with us. If we remain obedient to Him, He has a plan in mind to not only prosper us but others as well. Later, when Joseph had an opportunity to help his family, he was able to declare to his brothers: "But as for you, you meant evil against me; but God meant it for good, in order to bring it about as it is this day, to save many people alive" (Gen. 50:20 NKJV).

Memory Verse

Day by day the LORD takes care of the innocent,
and they will receive an inheritance that lasts forever.
They will not be disgraced in hard times;
even in famine they will have more than enough.
—Psalm 37:18–19 NLT

CHAPTER 2
Life Interrupted

Surviving Unexpected Tragedy

Storms continued to hammer the United States in 2017. Houston was hit by Hurricane Harvey, and at the time of this writing, Hurricane Maria had still left our Puerto Rican sisters and brothers without necessities such as running water and electricity. The cost of the devastation of these recent storms is still being calculated, but before these storms, Hurricane Katrina was recorded as the most destructive hurricane to strike the United States, and the costliest, causing $108 billion in damage, according to the National Oceanic and Atmospheric Administration (NOAA).[1]

By the time Hurricane Katrina struck New Orleans on Monday, August 29, it had already been raining heavily for hours. That morning Katrina swept over the Gulf Coast of the United States as a Category 3 rating on the Saffir-Simpson Hurricane Wind Scale. Aside from the abundance of rain, the hurricane brought sustained winds of 100 to 140 miles per hour and stretched some four hundred miles across. The storm itself did a great deal of damage, but its aftermath was catastrophic. New Orleans missed a direct hit from Katrina and instead the hurricane made landfall on the Mississippi Gulf Coast, where it caused severe destruction. It was the ensuing breach of the levee system that was responsible for most of the death and devastation in New Orleans. When the storm surge (as high as nine meters in some places) arrived, it overwhelmed many of the city's unstable levees and drainage canals. It was as if the wind-tattered city was sitting in a bowl of water.[2]

A 2015 *Live Science* article quoted Sandy Rosenthal, an American civic activist who founded the group Levees.org soon after Hurricane Katrina in order to educate the public about the reason for the levee failures and disastrous flooding in New Orleans. Rosenthal, a known critic of the Army Corps of Engineers, asserted, "The surge exposed engineering mistakes in the levees and floodwalls designed and built by the U.S. Army Corps of Engineers, causing extensive flooding throughout the New Orleans region."[3]

Those engineering issues resulted in catastrophic damage to the region as water seeped through the soil underneath some levees and swept others away altogether. By 9:00 a.m. on August 29, low-lying places like St. Bernard Parish and the Ninth Ward were under so much water that people had to scramble to attics and rooftops for safety. Another reason for the devastation was the number of people who could not escape the storm. Some 112,000 of New Orleans's nearly 500,000 people did not have access to a car.[4] Eventually, nearly 80 percent of the city was under some quantity of water.[5]

I can attest to the validity of the many statistics provided. The lower level of my own home was filled with fourteen feet of water. My family members also have horror stories from the days following the hurricane. My brother and his wife and children barely escaped the devastation in the Ninth Ward. As a result of the breach in the levee, their home was completely destroyed. My seventy-seven-year-old dad and stepmom, who had evacuated with my sister Sharon and her husband before the storm hit, went back to their shared New Orleans East home, which was in good shape until the levee broke. My dad had returned from the store and was in the kitchen when my nephew noticed that my dad's car was starting to fill up with water outside. Soon after that, the rising water levels began to come inside the house. My father and stepmom (who was on dialysis), along with my sister, her husband, and their children, had to escape to the over one-hundred-degree attic for three days to avoid drowning, as the water (seemingly from nowhere) filled their home. There was nowhere left to go. We could hear the devastation in my dad's voice as he shared the experience with us.

Although he was a war hero, because of the extreme heat, lack of drinking water, no phones, and no help in an evacuated area, my father said he thought for a moment they would all die in that attic. He could hear the helicopter come near my sister's house, but it never came to rescue them. Finally, his son-in-law hammered through the roof until he opened a small hole just large enough to push a broken compact mirror through. My father told me he felt it in his heart when on that third day the rescuers saw that little mirror reflection. Although the rescuers had left the area days before without seeing or hearing them, on day three of my family being in the attic, they came back and rescued my dad and my sister's family via helicopter. There was something about that third day, just like the resurrection story.

Before the storm, nearly 30 percent of New Orleans children lived in poverty. Katrina intensified and worsened these conditions by leaving many of New Orleans's most impoverished even more vulnerable than they had been before the storm. Additionally, the devastation of the storm was not restricted to socioeconomic effects; it also entailed emotional ones. According to the *New York Times*, surveys completed in the first seven years after Katrina revealed that "the rate of diagnosable mental health problems in the New Orleans area jumped by 9 percent—a sharper spike than after other natural disasters—and the effects did not discriminate much between race or income."[6] That's another statistic I lived. My mom, who had Alzheimer's, was in a nursing facility, and my sister was in another facility for mental illness. Both facilities had to evacuate.

For a long time, I had no way to find out where they were, but I had an overwhelming sense of peace that they were safe. Although I had no way of knowing for sure, because of the Holy Spirit's calming presence I maintained a peace that surpassed my limited human understanding.

As pastors, my husband and I lost many members to either forced relocation or, worse, death, especially among the elderly. In all, Hurricane Katrina killed nearly two thousand people and affected some ninety thousand square miles of the United States. Hundreds of thousands of those evacuees were scattered far and wide. Katrina evacuees fled to states all across the country, but the most substantial number went to Texas. Some resettled in cities like Houston and Austin; others returned to New Orleans. Large numbers of evacuees also relocated to Atlanta and Baton Rouge.[7] According to NOAA, it was one of the most massive displacements of a population since the Great Depression, and the Data Center, an independent research organization in New Orleans, found that the storm displaced more than one million people in the Gulf Coast region.[8] While many of the tourist areas, such as the French Quarter, have recovered, there are still neighborhoods just a short ride from the city that have completely vanished forever. At the foot of Canal Street, a local funeral home built a monument that lists the names of hundreds who died without a decent burial.

Storm Grade System

If this is your first time reading about this storm, I know it can be a lot to take in. It was a lot for those of us who survived it. However, for me, it was not the worst storm I had ever experienced. I want to give you your first strategy for successful storm survival. It is *grade your storms.*

We live in a time where social media firestorms can create almost instant crises. Unfortunately, the event that starts the crisis does not even have to be real. NBC's super popular show *This Is Us* created a PR crisis for Newell Brands, the makers of the Crock-Pot. A character on the show died as a result of a faulty Crock-Pot. Mass hysteria broke out, and people began throwing their Crock-Pots away and removing the item from wedding registry lists, according to WGRZ News.[9]

Now, as sad as the episode was, it was not real. We live in a time where the line between reality and fiction can become blurred pretty quickly. Newell Brands reached out to the cast of the show to help them calm viewers down and the crisis was averted, but it is remarkable how quickly the panic spread.

In our everyday lives, situations cannot be fixed with a press release, celebrity appeals and endorsements, or a Twitter campaign. In real life, we have to understand what constitutes a storm for us. A life event that makes me cry might make you angry enough to fight; perception indeed makes up the individual's reality. Although all storms take something away, I have learned they can also leave behind something invaluable.

For me, when Katrina hit, although it was an earth-shattering experience, it was not the worst storm of my life. That plane ride through Hurricane Katrina wasn't new. My Category 5 storm had already happened. One night thirteen years earlier, my husband and I flew through another storm to get to my daughter and son-in-law. Their daughter, my first grandbaby, had been admitted to the hospital for a virus, but after only an hour and a half there she died unexpectedly. We lost her at eighteen months old. It was one of the most painful experiences I'd ever had, and it left me in a state of numbness. Grandparents know what I mean. I felt dead inside. There was nothing I could do to bring her back. My grandbaby was gone. I was confused, angry, and filled with grief.

There are five stages of grief in the Kübler-Ross model: denial, anger, bargaining, depression, and acceptance. I felt like I was going through the first four continually, almost as if I were stuck on a merry-go-round. Eventually, though, I was able to arrive at acceptance through my faith and prayers and the grace and power of God. After I survived that Category 5, losing my dream home was not even a Category 3 to me. When my children would comfort me about the loss of my house, I would say, "I don't care about that. I'm glad we are all safe." I think they thought I had lost my mind, but I was serious.

There were people who were missing loved ones and didn't know if they'd ever see them again. I could empathize because it had taken me a while to locate my elderly aunt. So many older people died during the storm; stranded in care facilities, many just could not get out. As I said, my dad had evacuated but returned to the city as soon as the storm was over. Those of us who had lived in New Orleans all our lives believed that when hurricanes were over, they were completely over and it was safe to return. When my dad arrived at my sister's house, he quickly realized that was a bad idea. No one had expected the levee to break.

Although outside it was sunny and hot, in a short time there was water everywhere. Though my family was eventually rescued, so many others were not as fortunate.

Managing to make it out of the storm with our family intact was a great miracle. I know families who are still spread out after Katrina, and even though they now know where everyone is, they had to wait months before they even found their family members. The level of unrest, uncertainty, and disconnection for many people was unbearable. The displacement of one million people is a Category 5 storm—at least it was in the lives of those families. But losing my granddaughter has been so painful to me that losing furniture and a house meant nothing in comparison. I can replace those material possessions, but I can't replace my loved ones.

I learned that life is the most precious gift. As long as we are alive, we can reboot and start all over, from scratch if necessary. I was distressed for other people after Hurricane Katrina, but I wasn't sad for myself because losing a grandchild to a virus was the most horrifying, heartbreaking tragedy I'd ever experienced—it changed my "crisis scale." As long as I had breath in my body, God, and my family, nothing else could rock me to the core.

I challenge you to take out that notebook or journal you have been keeping and create your own scale. Take a look at the effects in the natural realm of each storm category, based on the Saffir-Simpson Hurricane Wind Scale:

- **Category 1:** You can expect winds to range from 74 to 95 miles per hour, and they can be expected to cause some minor damage to property. Injuries to humans and animals can also occur because of isolated falling debris.

- **Category 2:** You can expect winds to range from 96 to 110 miles per hour, causing extensive property damage. These wind speeds heighten the risk of injury because of more debris and structural damage to buildings. There will likely be flooding in low-lying areas, widespread power outages, and, in many cases, water filtration systems failure.
- **Category 3:** You can expect winds ranging from 111 to 130 miles per hour, causing significant damage to property, animals, and humans. Poorly constructed homes will be destroyed, and well-built structures will still sustain damage. Extensive inland flooding is more likely with a Category 3, and water and electricity are often unavailable for weeks after this kind of storm.
- **Category 4:** You can expect winds to range from 131 to 155 miles per hour, causing catastrophic damage to property, animals, and humans. All types of buildings are vulnerable to structural damage, and water and electricity shortages can last from many weeks to many months.
- **Category 5:** You can expect winds at or greater than 155 miles per hour, causing catastrophic damage to property, animals, and humans. This storm will cause the complete or almost-complete destruction of mobile homes, frame homes, apartments, and shopping centers, and almost all trees in the affected area will be snapped or uprooted. Power outages and water shortages can last for weeks and possibly months, and most of the affected area will be uninhabitable for weeks or months.[10]

Now, as you read these categories, think about your own life. For one person, a Category 1 may be a promotion denial. You may have wanted that job, but being passed over for the position is not going to cause any real damage. You will apply again or maybe even somewhere else.

A Category 2 may be the demise of a friendship that you thought would last forever. It hurts, but you will recover, even if it takes some time.

A Category 3 may be contracting a sickness that is curable but having to fight it, like some forms of cancer. That storm is attacking and seeking to destroy you, but you can get to safety and ride it out. It may be tough for weeks or months as you endure treatments and expensive medications, but in the end you will survive.

A Category 4 may be a devastating divorce. When two people marry, the Bible says they become one flesh,[11] so to divorce can feel like literally ripping away a body part. If you have children, it may be even worse, depending on how they cope and what storm level the breakup is for them. If it uproots them and takes them to a new school and away from familiar surroundings and friends, for them it may be a Category 5.

The levels of devastation for you are what define a storm for your life. It is okay if your storm grades are different from someone else's. The crisis for one person is not the same as another's. I did not throw my Crock-Pot away after that *This Is Us* episode, but I understand the genuine feelings of the individuals who did.

If you can grade it, you can assess the storm's impact on you. If you can determine the impact, you can do what you need to do to clean up the debris from it. You can also seek help from a neighbor to assist you in cleaning up after the storm. Additionally, you may opt to seek out higher elevation with a seasoned storm survivor who can help you with the storm you are experiencing.

Unfortunately, you will find that storms change your life

forever. New Orleans changed forever after Katrina. Even after extensive rebuilding, certain aspects of the city will never be the same. I survived my granddaughter's passing, but I will never be the same. There is something missing from my life I can never replace. However, I let these storms teach me powerful lessons that I can now pass along to you.

Grade your storms, because there is more work for you to do and a greater life awaiting you than anything you have lost or left behind. You need to be committed to doing the work to manifest your healing, grasp your purpose, and move passionately toward your destiny! I am cheering you on all the way. Now that we have learned about our storms and the importance of grading them, let's talk about growing from them.

Storm Playbook Study

Chapter Summary
- Be aware that storms affect everyone differently.
- Never give up, even when the situation looks hopeless and dead; we serve a God who often shows up symbolically on the "third day."
- All storms are not alike. Grading your storms can help you apply the best preventative and restorative measures.

Journaling
1. What storms have you already weathered in your life? Write them in your journal, and next to each storm, grade them according to the scale provided in this chapter.
2. What did each storm teach you?

Storm Survivor: Ruth

Our next storm survivor, Ruth, a woman of the country of Moab, is remarkable for a few reasons. Ruth became a widow as a young woman. Losing your spouse is tough at any age, especially if it's unexpected. When Naomi, Ruth's mother-in-law, chose to return to Israel, her homeland, after her husband and both her sons had died, Ruth and her sister-in-law, Orpah, followed after her, saying they would go with her, but Naomi protested:

> "Turn back, my daughters; why will you go with me? Are there still sons in my womb, that they may be your husbands? Turn back, my daughters, go—for I am too old to have a husband. If I should say I have hope, if I should have a husband tonight and should also bear sons, would you wait for them till they were grown? Would you restrain yourselves from having husbands? No, my daughters; for it grieves me very much for your sakes that the hand of the LORD has gone out against me!"

Then they lifted up their voices and wept again; and Orpah kissed her mother-in-law, but Ruth clung to her.

And she said, "Look, your sister-in-law has gone back to her people and to her gods; return after your sister-in-law."

But Ruth said:

> "Entreat me not to leave you,
> Or to turn back from following after you;
> For wherever you go, I will go;
> And wherever you lodge, I will lodge;
> Your people shall be my people,
> And your God, my God.
> Where you die, I will die,

And there will I be buried.
The LORD do so to me, and more also,
If anything but death parts you and me." (Ruth
1:11–17 NKJV)

Ruth made an unconventional choice; she remained loyal to her mother-in-law, Naomi, who was so melancholy she renamed herself Mara to reflect the overwhelming bitterness she felt. But Ruth decided to return to her mother-in-law's land, where she would be a foreigner and looked down upon due to her heritage, so that she could help care for Naomi.

Ruth is a wonderful reminder that God can take a storm and "relocate" you to a better situation and overall better life. Ruth immediately received favor upon arriving in her new country. I suggest you read the entire book of Ruth (it is only four chapters). Ruth became the wife of one of Naomi's kinsmen, and both women ended up living a biblical happily ever after.

Memory Verse

Consider it pure joy, my brothers and sisters, whenever you face trials of many kinds, because you know that the testing of your faith produces perseverance. Let perseverance finish its work so that you may be mature and complete, not lacking anything.

—James 1:2–4

CHAPTER 3
Maturity

Mandatory Growth

Every individual has a decision to make when faced with a storm in their life. While storms will always occur, it is the individual's choice whether to learn from them. Too often a storm happens and the person stays the same. These situations often lead to the person facing cycles of very similar tests or storms until they change their reaction to it. In my line of work, I consistently meet people from all walks of life. So many people end up living mediocre lives after their storms because they refuse to learn and grow from them.

One area where you will repeatedly be challenged in life is the area of relationships. One day recently I was walking to my car, and a young lady from my office joined me and started telling me about a situation with her car. I asked her what had happened to it, and she described in depth how her new boyfriend had gotten into some trouble with the law. When the authorities caught up with him, he was driving her car; they took him, and her car was impounded. Being a mom, I had a lot of questions (such as: Why are you dating a criminal and allowing him to drive your vehicle? Is this the only guy available?), but I refrained from asking them because she was not family. As I listened, I realized that sometimes people make poor choices when it pertains to romantic relationships. I can give you another example.

Once, a young lady came into my office crying because her

boyfriend of several years had suddenly left. Shortly after his disappearance, she discovered that pictures of him with another girl were all over social media. The saddest part is she never saw it coming. Her life now in shambles, she was devastated and a complete wreck. As sad as her story is, it is not even the worst one I have heard.

Another young lady I knew, a highly intelligent woman with three degrees and the ability to speak two languages, was almost homeless after marrying a man who had presented himself as the perfect guy. She later found out that during that time he was still married with a wife and three kids. Their whole relationship was a lie. Nothing prepared her for that level of hurt and pain.

Many times relationships fail because we let them replace our relationship with God. We begin to not trust in Him when other relationships come along offering us natural fulfillment. We don't admit it because we are unaware of Satan's tactics. He is subtle but destructive. He disguises himself with compliments, flattery, and companionship. Some people struggle because of terrible childhood experiences, bouts of rejection, and broken spirits. Satan enters in through those open wounds and causes people to seek false fulfillment from false gods who make compelling promises that disguise deceit. They promise rewards they cannot fulfill.

Our relationship with God will cause us to have more honest and fruitful relationships. I've discovered that at the root of my relationships I must understand that God is good and God is love. If I stay connected to Him, I can experience healthy, long-lasting relationships, whereas relationships where Satan is in the midst will eventually disappoint us and God! We see the evidence of deceit and disappointment in a relationship in Genesis 3:1–7.

The serpent was the shrewdest of all the wild animals the LORD God had made. One day he asked the woman, "Did God really say you must not eat the fruit from any of the trees in the garden?"

"Of course we may eat fruit from the trees in the garden," the woman replied. "It's only the fruit from the tree in the middle of the garden that we are not allowed to eat. God said, 'You must not eat it or even touch it; if you do, you will die.'"

"You won't die!" the serpent replied to the woman. "God knows that your eyes will be opened as soon as you eat it, and you will be like God, knowing both good and evil."

The woman was convinced. She saw that the tree was beautiful and its fruit looked delicious, and she wanted the wisdom it would give her. So she took some of the fruit and ate it. Then she gave some to her husband, who was with her, and he ate it, too. At that moment their eyes were opened, and they suddenly felt shame at their nakedness. So they sewed fig leaves together to cover themselves. (NLT)

God designed the earth with the intent that mankind would enjoy it and live to the full. The very first man and woman, Adam and Eve, were created in His image and then blessed to rule and have authority over all the good things He had made and provided for them to live a good life. However, we must . . .

Beware of Satan's Tactics

Satan does not want us to enjoy life or one another. His goal is to insert, in our minds and hearts, doubt and mistrust in one another and eventually disappointment, failure, and shame.

Satan uses his influence to make us desire to know as much or more than God, just as he did with Eve. That way we will not consult God for a mate or for answers about the mate we already have, but instead choose to go our own way. Eventually our own smarts will come back to haunt us. We will realize Satan's direction was wrong and caused a negative impact in our life. In our world today, we have more information than ever, yet we also have more broken relationships and lonely people than ever, and, consequently, more broken families. Satan has caused man to move further and further away from God. For millions of people, it seems that life will never get better. During and after a storm, we can be at our most vulnerable, but if through prayer and meditation we make ourselves more aware of Satan's tactics, we can affect this world in a positive way by our healthy relationships.

Toxic, evil, or negative conversation is a sure sign that Satan is present and trying to cause conflict. He did it to Eve. He makes you question the right thing you are doing. He also makes you suspicious of other people's good deeds. Trust is a huge part of healthy relationships; when it is absent, the relationship becomes a burden.

Conversations with Satan are not always as evident as was Eve's. Satan is not a snake or a serpent on its belly. Satan may look very beautiful or handsome, but the conversations are void of what's good and truthful. He tells partial truths in order to deceive. People don't come crawling on their belly, but they can indeed be snakes. Beware. For instance, a guy once asked me if I was married. I said, "Yes, for many years." His next question was, "But are you happy?" I knew immediately it was Satan talking. Even if I was not happy, God would not use that angle to help me. Marriage is honorable, so there are no buts. Sure, we will have problems in relationships, but we should seek godly counsel: "The godly offer good counsel; they teach right from wrong" (Ps. 37:30 NLT).

———

Through spending time with God and His Word, we begin to grow in our understanding of the Creator as well as to engage in and cultivate more mature and healthy relationships. Too many people are underdeveloped spiritually and emotionally. Hebrews 5:14 says, "But solid food is for the mature—for those whose senses have been trained to distinguish between good and evil" (CSB).

We must realize we have a spirit that lives in a body and possesses a soul. You must have a spiritual connection with the One who created you in order to understand how you tick. This knowledge will, in turn, help balance your emotions. Why? We will not react so quickly to what people say, especially untruths, because we will be more in touch with our truth: "And ye shall know the truth, and the truth shall make you free" (John 8:32 KJV).

We must know ourselves or we will deceive our own selves. When we don't know our own soul and our deep desires (perhaps for attention or fame), we can be enticed into wrong relationships. When we're weak, we cause others to be weak. That is what happened with Eve. She was enticed by the opportunity to have more knowledge about life, so she ate the forbidden fruit. The sad thing is that she caused another person to fall as well. In that kind of relationship, no one thrives.

Spiritual Maturity Will Be the Result of Connecting to God's Spirit

"And be not drunk with wine, wherein is excess; but be filled with the Spirit" (Eph. 5:18 KJV). Let me offer an explanation for this scripture. As we connect with God's Spirit and allow Him to flow through us—mind, body, and emotions—He will help train our senses to distinguish between good and evil, and you will be able to use this training in your own relationships as well as help others experience the same. We need more wise teachers in our world.

There are many types of storms that are proven to test our maturity.

1. Facing career and/or business difficulty.

Few things mature you like taking a severe financial hit. Think about it: no one escapes the IRS indefinitely. Tax debts catch up with you. I know a young man who didn't file a tax return for seven years. Now he will be paying more to the IRS for the next fifteen years because he owes $50,000 in back taxes. It was immaturity that made him think he could evade the federal government forever.

Sometimes the financial decisions made in our youth can have devastating consequences later in life. For example, Americans are drowning in student loan debt.[1] Many people borrowed more money than they needed and used the excess to "live large." Others stayed in school and took out loans because they didn't know what career path to follow or because they simply didn't want to get a job. Of course, for-profit colleges and climbing tuition rates have contributed to the problem, but being smart with choosing a college helps. College is a time for getting an education that creates a solid career foundation; it should not be a time to accrue debt.

Negative career choices and failed business ventures also test maturity. I have counseled individuals who hop from job to job and wonder why they cannot move up the corporate ladder. I know people who are so fed up with their nine-to-five that they quit their job and prematurely start a business that fails because of poor planning and no capital. Poor business decisions happen at every level. On a larger scale, bad business deals create losses that force the company to restructure, which usually leads to massive layoffs.

As devastating as all these situations can be, when people's pocketbooks or wallets suffer enough hits, they change their financial decision making. For example, think about the first time a prospective homebuyer has their credit score pulled only to find out they don't have a high enough score required to close the deal. That person is devastated, but often they find that was the push they needed to change their spending and bill-paying patterns.

2. Parenting.

I can say without a doubt that few things challenge a person's maturity like having a child. Having children is one of the most significant, life-changing decisions a person can make, but there are no requirements or special certifications needed to have a baby. Maturity is needed when you bring a life into the world because you are now tasked with taking care of someone who is dependent solely on you. You should live a little differently, being conscious that you have someone who is looking to you as their example. Ultimately, children will do what you do and not what you say. Maturity causes you to recognize that you may not have all the answers, but you can work to find them. You look to more experienced parents whose parenting practices you respect for advice and strategies on how to be the best parent possible.

Proverbs 22:6 states, "Train up a child in the way he should go, and when he is old he will not depart from it" (NKJV). In the church world, we've viewed that scripture to mean that if you raise your children in the right way, regardless of the path they choose they will eventually come back to the "right way." I would like to submit a different point of view. Parents carry a grave responsibility to model appropriate behavior for their children so that they will be productive members of society, yet many parents do not understand the full weight of that responsibility. Children today are being raised without strong moral values and are instead being trained by their parents to pursue a life absent of morality. Based on the scripture, we can see why we have older adults still living lives of immorality; it is because they have not departed from the way in which they were trained. It works both ways.

After you learn these relational, financial, and parental lessons, you are now qualified to teach them to others. We are all called to be teachers. God designed us that way. There is always someone watching each of us, whether we want them to or not. So learn the lesson and then be the teacher. A side benefit is that once you learn the lesson, you don't have to retake the test. There is nothing worse than repeating a grade because you did not learn the material. You want to make sure you don't repeat unproductive cycles in your life because you refuse to learn the lesson offered.

Now it is time to recover from the painful event that put you in the situation in the first place. Let's talk about how you do just that.

Steps for Recovering from a Storm

I have shared some of my experiences that occurred right after Hurricane Katrina. Now I want to share steps to help you cope as you work toward recovering from the storms that have hit your life.

1. Heed the warnings.

When you are mature, you don't have to be told something repeatedly. You can be warned instead of having to go through each trial firsthand. So many difficulties could be avoided if we would only listen to the advice or instruction that we are given the first time. During Katrina, we had people who suffered because they had the means to leave the city and did not. They felt they knew better than the professionals. If you are going to take that kind of risk, you must be sure you are correct. There is an excellent example of this in the 2004 hit movie *Million Dollar Baby*. Margaret "Maggie" Fitzgerald, played by Hilary Swank, a waitress and wannabe boxer from the Missouri Ozarks, shows up in the Hit Pit, a run-down gym in Los Angeles operated by Frankie Dunn, an ornery boxing trainer, played by Clint Eastwood.

Frankie refuses to train Maggie at first but eventually is won over by her skill and her ability to fill the paternal hole in his heart left by his estranged daughter. She gets good at boxing and wins a bunch of fights. Then she gets challenged to go up against a German fighter with a reputation of fighting dirty, nicknamed Billie "the Blue Bear." Frankie knows instantly that this fight is a bad idea. He tries to discourage Maggie from accepting the challenge, but they proceed. Although the match begins with a rough start for Maggie, during the fight she starts to gain the upper hand. When Billie realizes that she will not beat Maggie fair and square, she hits Maggie with an illegal sucker punch. Maggie falls, landing so that she breaks her neck, which leaves her paralyzed.

My point in sharing this example is, no matter if it is a Category 3 storm or a boxing match with a dirty-playing opponent, there are some risks you shouldn't take. None of you would let an unrepentant, unapologetic killer live in your house. It is not wise and too big of a risk. You must strive to heighten your discernment and operate in wisdom to avoid these kinds of pitfalls. The most painless recoveries are the ones you don't have to make because you made a quality decision instead.

2. Take time to assess the situation.

There is absolutely no way to know just how detrimental a challenge may be at first glance. You must learn to take the time to investigate the situations that come into your life and assess them correctly. Every problem you face is not a negative one. Some incidents help us grow up. Some circumstances help us know the people who are negative influences and therefore need to be eliminated from our circle. It is incredible to me how so many of us are just like Little Red Riding Hood and can't tell the difference between Grandma and the Big Bad Wolf—even when in the back of our minds we know something is not right and we are uncomfortable with the situation. Let's be clear: as Christians, we know that the Holy Spirit warns us if something is not right. We will avoid some horrible pitfalls if we listen to Him. For every potentially harmful situation, He gives us an escape plan.

First Corinthians 10:13 declares, "There hath no temptation taken you but such as is common to man: but God is faithful, who will not suffer you to be tempted above that ye are able;

but will with the temptation also make a way to escape, that ye may be able to bear it" (KJV). The temptations are the situations we face in our lives that help us assess where we are as believers. Be assured that every obstacle, every opportunity to make the wrong decision, is coupled with an escape plan.

The Holy Spirit is talking all the time, but are you heeding His voice? He helps you look at the situation with a fresh perspective. He lets you see the way to escape so you can bear the consequences of your decision. He shows us the way to get out of a potentially adverse situation *every time.* We all can look back on an act we engaged in that had negative consequences and determine the exact time when we could have made a different choice.

One of the best ways to ensure that you are able to see a situation clearly is to get enough sleep on a regular basis, but not so much sleep that you are not accomplishing anything. Think about when an infant is born—sleep is the thing they do the most to grow strong and remain healthy. They sleep most of the day, and, unfortunately for most parents, almost not at all at night. Know that you need the proper amount of rest to aid you in your assessment process. Don't forget: as humans we are mind, body, and spirit. Oh, and you are not Superman or Wonder Woman!

3. Create an action plan for your next steps.

New Year's resolutions often do not work because they are ideas without action plans. If you are going to produce anything, you will have to create a plan to bring it to fruition.

Farming is a great example of the need for planning. There are seasons to plant, and there are seasons to harvest. If you don't know the seasons, then you cannot execute the steps it will take to produce the crop you want. The same is true for many things in life. So many people struggle to achieve greatness because they were not thinking about greatness in the proper season. So many students decide they want to get serious about their coursework at the end of the season, and typically that is too late. If you wait to find out which courses you need for your transcript when you are already a junior in high school, there is a good possibility you will not have enough time left to take the courses necessary to gain entrance into college.

When you have an idea, you must take the time to sit down and create an action plan to make it happen. This plan must contain goals with action items and due dates. Without due dates, your goals on the paper are just ideas. The due dates place a written demand on you to produce results by a set time. If you want to take it one step further, use technology. Use your calendar on your smartphone or tablet to create to-do lists and set alarms and reminders. I had to learn this lesson the hard way. By not writing things down, I would rely on my memory (bad) or the Holy Spirit (missed Him too), and consequently I missed some great opportunities.

I frequently recall that during and after Katrina, I thanked God that my husband had a plan for our family. He was very clear on when to leave the city and where to go, even though I had originally wanted to wait out the storm on the second floor of the house. Immediately after the storm, his emotions and compassion kicked in, which was admirable, and he went to several cities, comforting the people. Eventually, though, he heard God tell him to settle down and feed His sheep. He had gone to Houston, Memphis, and Baton Rouge, but God said Atlanta and

New Orleans were to be his focus, even though our home was destroyed in New Orleans.

Our children and grandchildren were with us in Atlanta, staying with different friends and spiritual family members. We had no permanent place to stay, but we were happy. We were being encouraged and blessed by them each day. As the plan fully unfolded, we could see the hand of God. A few weeks after the storm, to reestablish a sense of normalcy, my husband and I leased an apartment. My eldest daughter and her family did the same, and we made sure we were near each other. Family support was very important to maintain. Simultaneously, we found a place to jumpstart our ministry in Atlanta. We became one church in two states; God had enlarged our territory.

We plan in the natural realm as much as possible and ask God's wisdom and blessings to be with us, but He can always override our plan to enlarge our territory. No need to try to convince anyone that it is a good plan. The proof is in the pudding. Believers were added to the new ministry weekly.

4. Enlist the tools and people you need (if applicable) to assist in executing the plan.

Now that you have a plan, you need to build a team to help you manifest it.

This team should fill your gaps. You don't need a team of people who are just like you and think just like you. That will not help you. In fact, it will only frustrate you in the long run. It may be fun in the beginning because you agree with each other, but it turns into a challenge when a ball gets dropped in an area where you are both weak. You must staff your weaknesses and not your strengths. This is a major key that you really cannot grasp until you are mature. When you are immature, you want familiarity, and you may fear others will get the credit for the success of your plan. However, when you are mature, you are comfortable with situations and people who are different from you. As you mature and prepare to really go after success in a serious way, you make sure you have every single item and team member you need.

In *The 17 Indisputable Laws of Teamwork*, John C. Maxwell wrote about the Law of the Niche, which says that each person on a team needs to be chosen carefully for their particular position based on their strengths and qualifications.[2] In order to do that, you must be able to accurately assess your team. Having that knowledge is great, but you then must have the wisdom to correctly position each member to maximize their strengths and eclipse their deficiencies. The goal is to set up each team member for success. All "dream teams" are built with the team members' strengths and weaknesses in mind. It should be a win-win for all parties involved.

Never set yourself or a member of your team up for failure by putting demands on a skill that is lacking. Many times I've found that it is difficult to help others deal with their weaknesses. However, we must care enough not to want to see them fail (although sometimes that's the only way they will grow). As a teacher in life, you must learn to gently but still forcefully massage them into their right place. It's like a good massage therapist who digs in to those tight areas to loosen the muscles so they can work properly. It hurts, and after the massage you may be sore, but you definitely feel better. You think, *That was good pain!* Through your help, your team members will discover their "sweet spot."

5. Make prayer or meditation and physical exercise a part of your recovery.

The truth is you will thrive after tragedy much faster by making these a part of your weekly routine, and I recommend incorporating them in that order.

Prayer is important. Taking time to talk to God, and to listen to what He wants to tell you, is so crucial. It is a two-way conversation, figuratively speaking. Psalm 145:18 says, "The LORD is nigh unto all them that call upon him, to all that call upon him in truth" (KJV). He is waiting to hear from you. He already knows the truth about you, but He wants you to tell Him that truth. Once you talk to Him in truth, He speaks truth back to you. Don't do all of the talking. Speak to Him and wait for a response. He says in the Word, "Be still, and know that I am God" (Ps. 46:10 KJV). Additionally, reading your Bible and allowing the Word to minister to you is critical because many times He speaks to us directly through His Word.

Now, if you are skeptical or new to prayer, you should create a time for quiet and peaceful meditation. You can find an isolated location and get away from your emails, calls, and responsibilities. Create opportunities for your mind to reset.

Jesus was very close to the family of Lazarus and his two sisters. Once when Jesus was visiting, Martha was working hard around the house and was annoyed that Mary was not helping her but was instead sitting at Jesus' feet. In response to Martha's complaint, Jesus said, "Martha, Martha, thou art careful and troubled about many things: But one thing is needful: and Mary hath chosen that good part, which shall not be taken away from her" (Luke 10:41–42 KJV).

This is such a powerful lesson for life. Mary was sitting at

Jesus' feet, listening. Many people hear but do not have good listening skills. We must discipline ourselves to slow down and sit down to get divine direction from God. I'm sure you've discovered by now that you don't have all the answers. You don't have the whole plan, so open yourself to listen to the One who has the missing pieces to make your plan work. Now you are #winning.

After prayer, I highly recommend that you get serious about exercise or increasing your physical activity. Studies show that sitting for long periods of time is so harmful some companies have invested in desks that workers use standing up. I watched a TED talk where an executive officer requires her teams to have walking meetings. The team has the meeting walking across their business campus. It helps with attentiveness, creativity, and overall health.[3] Pre-Katrina at a doctor's visit, I asked my doctor for his opinion on why the number of cancer cases has increased in the world. From his thirty years of practicing medicine, he felt that lack of exercise was one of the most significant factors. Shocked, I asked, "Not poor nutrition?" He said diet was significant, but more so was the lack of exercise.

That conversation changed my life, and I then decided to share his advice with others. So if you really want to see an improvement in your overall well-being, you should also consider adjusting your exercise and nutrition habits. You will find yourself feeling better, moving faster, and thinking more clearly. All these things are necessary if you want to achieve a greater level of maturity. Now that I have given you some tools to help you grow and mature, let's talk about finding strength in the storm's aftermath.

Storm Playbook Study

Chapter Summary

- Don't just go through the storm. Grow through it.
- Often storms repeat in our lives when we do not learn important lessons from them the first time.
- Three areas where storms can reoccur are relationships, finances, and parenting; these storms create pathways for maturity.
- Storms are often preceded by warnings. Be sure to heed them.

Journaling

1. In what ways have you matured because of the storms in your life? In what area(s) do you still need to grow?
2. Which of the recovery steps do you most need to work on? How and when will you begin incorporating it into your life?

Storm Survivor: Queen Esther

The story of Queen Esther is one of my favorite stories of thriving after a storm. Xerxes, the king at that time, was humiliated by his wife, who refused to come out and show her beauty to his intoxicated friends. At his friends' urging, she was dismissed as queen, lest she influence other wives to be disobedient. However, it was the will of God to get Esther into the position of queen.

At the recommendation of her cousin Mordecai, who raised her, Esther entered the contest to select a new queen. Among all

the contestants, Esther found favor with the caretaker of the contestants and was chosen by the king. Months after she became
queen, she faced a storm.

Esther received word that Mordecai was reportedly sitting
outside the castle in a sackcloth. When Esther inquired what
was wrong, he sent her a message saying that Haman, one of the
king's men, had a plan to kill all the Jews and requested that she
entreat the king to save them.

> "All the king's officials and the people of the royal provinces
> know that for any man or woman who approaches the king
> in the inner court without being summoned the king has but
> one law: that they be put to death unless the king extends the
> gold scepter to them and spares their lives. But thirty days have
> passed since I was called to go to the king."
>
> When Esther's words were reported to Mordecai, he sent
> back this answer: "Do not think that because you are in the
> king's house you alone of all the Jews will escape. For if you
> remain silent at this time, relief and deliverance for the Jews
> will arise from another place, but you and your father's family
> will perish. And who knows but that you have come to your
> royal position for such a time as this?"
>
> Then Esther sent this reply to Mordecai: "Go, gather together
> all the Jews who are in Susa, and fast for me. Do not eat or drink
> for three days, night or day. I and my attendants will fast as you
> do. When this is done, I will go to the king, even though it is
> against the law. And if I perish, I perish." (Est. 4:11–16)

Just in case you are not familiar with the story of Esther
(spoiler alert), she does not perish. As a matter of fact, not only

are Esther and Mordecai's people saved, but the king executes justice on Haman, the villain of this story.

Esther is a great example of fighting fear and walking by faith during a stormy situation. Although Esther was a young queen, she was forced to mature and take action quickly. Her people were in danger, and the only way she could help would put her own life at risk. In spite of facing death, she went before the king, made her requests known, and set forth a plan to also eliminate the man who was a threat to her people.

There are storms in our lives that we face as the result of harm done to us by others. This story reminds us that vengeance is action best left to God. He can vindicate us better than we can vindicate ourselves.

Storm Song

Esther's victory makes me think of a Storm Song that I would like you to find and download on your favorite music platform, "Reckless Love" by Cory Asbury.

My favorite line is, "There's no lie you won't tear down coming after me." At some point in your life, you will face an injustice. Just know that we serve a God who exposes evil and vindicates His righteous children.

Memory Verse

When I was a child, I talked like a child, I thought like a child, I reasoned like a child. When I became a man, I put the ways of childhood behind me.

—1 Corinthians 13:11

CHAPTER 4

Finding Strength in the Aftermath

After you are on the road to recovery, it is crucial to build upon that foundation of maturity and change. If you do not immediately start to build on it, you will find yourself stagnating or, worse, regressing.

Once you reach a certain level of maturity, you will notice new strengths emerge. I discovered a new strength after Hurricane Katrina.

One day my husband and I met with some of our employees and contractors to start the rebuilding process for our church. A few weeks later, once we began reconstruction, my husband asked, "Dee, you got this?"

He was asking me if I could handle overseeing the construction. His request shocked me because he had never asked me to run any portion of a building project before. This devastating storm had cleared a path for me to play a new role. Designing was a passion I had always had, so I took it seriously and was excited about the new opportunity. In retrospect, doing this also allowed me to develop my administrative and organizational skills.

This was part of my personal recovery and rebuilding process too. In it, I learned a precious lesson: sometimes it takes a storm to expose your strengths. In other instances, it may take a storm to expand your skill set. Regardless of which way you look at it, once the new gifts are discovered, you have an opportunity to grab hold of the new thing that arises out of the devastation. In Scripture, God says, "I will do a new thing." I have learned that this is especially true after a storm. He then asks, "Shall you not know it?" (Isa. 43:19 NKJV). You must ask yourself, "Can He do a new thing in me?" You must realize that He is willing and capable, but He needs your permission. Will you allow Him to reshape your life and stir new passion within you, or will you drown in old waters that have long passed over? It is your choice. I'm rooting for you!

The key is to use your insight rather than only your eyesight. If you do, there will always be something positive gained in any situation. For me, using "insight over eyesight" meant stretching myself in a new area. It was difficult at first, because in the natural realm our building was destroyed, but mentally and spiritually I was expanding into a new area of life: business and ministry with my husband and the others he entrusted with the project. Choosing to see and begin work on the "new thing" and the next thing is vital to living through the aftermath of a storm.

The aftermath presents you with a type of two-way mirror. It shows you who you were before the storm, and it shows you who you are now. If you seize this moment, you can begin to pursue a newly uncovered purpose and rebuild the areas of your life that were devastated by the storm.

During and after Katrina and other storms, God began to give me insight, or revelation, about the storm. Our thinking and understanding are limited in the natural realm, but supernaturally God's Holy Spirit will give us greater insight into situations in order to help us heal and grow. He will use His gifts in us to help us receive understanding to brighten our path and also, even more important and phenomenal, to help so many others. I have a prophetic and teaching gift that God uses to help others. What gift or gifts has God given you to help make things better for others?

God revealed that the stormwater of Katrina was like the solution doctors use to cleanse and remove the dirt from an infected eye in order to do two things: to see the real issues and to cause them to be corrected. If He hadn't sent the waters, many people wouldn't have known the underlying issues that were plaguing their lives. Not dirt in the eye, but some serious issues on every level of leadership and citizenship. Some said it was because of the sin in the city of New Orleans. Well, since then we have seen storms hit many states and cities. Sin is everywhere, but God gives revelation and insight. What the devil means for evil God turns into a blessing for those who receive the insight.

After Katrina, many people received new homes, better education, and better lives in general; others stayed the same or got worse. It all depended on their positive or negative responses to the storm lessons. God may have told them, "Move away from old and familiar places, people, and things," like He told Abraham, who obeyed and got blessed. Many don't obey and then don't get blessed. I am a true believer in that if we follow the insight God gives, we will thrive after any storm in life. We will also see purpose in it.

To me, an individual's personal rebuilding process is a very spiritual one. Regardless of religious beliefs, most people believe in the validity of a creator and a creation story. I have encountered very few individuals who do not believe in a higher power, even if they do not share my Christian faith and beliefs. Let me explain more. I believe that every person has a spirit that lives in a body and possesses a mind. Often people focus so much on the outer world and what's going on around them that they fail to pay attention to their inner worlds.

Our inner being is responsible for so much of our general well-being. Our psyche, mental state, and emotions are all affected by how we function and process life internally. Many times the elements of the outer world will control what happens to us internally. That's unfortunate, because what we see is temporary but what's inside can be eternal. In other words, what's within us can be more meaningful and lasting than the crazy events and circumstances that surround us. Consequently, every man and woman should get in touch with his or her spirit. Prioritizing that internal spiritual process yields clarity and peace. Aligning one's inner self creates the opportunity to understand who you genuinely are. Facing your reality makes it easier to accept that you are a summation of all you have suffered. It makes it easier to process past hurts and pains. When a person takes the time to deal with their past internally, it is much easier to heal. Healing causes us to go from figurative darkness into light, both physically and mentally.

To explain another way, imagine you have been kept in a dark cave for months. You have food, and you are not mistreated, but you just cannot see anything. Robbed of your sense of sight, the other senses become stronger, and you learn to focus on the ones you can use. The clues you have about what you are eating before you place something in your mouth are smell and touch. You would smell it to identify what it was, and you would touch it to see how to eat it. In the same way, after being freed from the darkness, your smell and touch would not be nearly as critical because your eyes could give you all the information you needed. This type of "sight" is important to surviving and recovering from storms, and it's important for shaping your perspective.

We need this insight because when storms come into our lives, they can leave us in a temporary state of blindness or severely impair our perspective. You must be intentional about regaining your sight and maintaining a positive attitude. Instead of accepting the challenge of overseeing our church's rebuilding campaign, I could have responded negatively to my husband. I could have been upset or resentful that he was giving me more work to do on top of everything I already needed to do at church and home. I could have tried to give the task to someone else. I could have just refused the assignment up front. But I didn't. I took on the responsibility and learned so many lessons that prepared me for future projects and events.

I learned that good administration is vitally important in overseeing a construction project. There are so many details that must be managed, and dropping the ball in one area could cause a domino effect in others. The ability to assess the skill sets of team members and delegate tasks appropriate for their skill level and commitment is vital. I learned that just because someone has a business card with a title on it doesn't necessarily mean they are competent in that line of work. My administrative capacity increased significantly.

I also learned that communication is critical. In construction, there are architects who draw up the plans, foremen or supervisors who assign the tasks, and workers who complete the tasks. If any of these individuals fail to communicate during the project, the results can be disastrous. I had to learn how to communicate with all of them and be sure that I hired a team of people who interacted well with one another.

This experience also expanded my leadership abilities. In addition to church leadership and ministry oversight, I learned to handle issues with contracts, permits, and local officials. I learned that nothing happens without an action plan with deadlines, and someone had to make sure there was a timeline and the schedule was kept.

The construction industry can be very stressful. It's male dominated, and I had to learn how to negotiate difficult situations without jeopardizing the project. There were also some answers I couldn't get from a book or the internet; I needed inner-sight. Often, when unfamiliar situations arise, you can find it easy to come up with a quick solution on your own. But as I have gotten older, I have learned to ask the Holy Spirit for help, and without fail I have always received the revelation I needed to solve the problem. Hallelujah! Again, the storm that caused so many challenges also afforded me so many great opportunities. It allowed me to find new strengths and apply them in the aftermath.

In addition to finding new strengths, I also had to assess my weaknesses. I learned very quickly the areas in which I needed development and then I sought to build them up. I did this in a few ways. First, I learned more about the subject where I had limited knowledge. We live in a time when it is easier than ever to access information and resources, so I took full advantage of seminars, books, and online articles.

Next, I realized there were some areas where I just needed help, so I began to surround myself with people who were well educated in the areas where I was weak. If you are not a good speller, then I suggest you find someone to proofread your memos or download software that edits for you. While you can improve your expertise in an area, it may be quicker and more efficient to obtain assistance from someone trained.

I learned that although I am a bargain hunter, sometimes being cheap will cost you more. When you are doing large projects, there are some components of construction where a generic brand will do, but there are instances where you will save more money in the long run by purchasing the higher-quality item up front. It is crucial to understand both your strengths and your weaknesses so that your imperfections don't severely hinder your progress.

Last, I found an inner strength in the storm's aftermath, which showed me that because I decided to see the storm with my "inner-sight" over my "eyesight," I could use my experience to pass this strength along to others. That is what inner strength does. It bears the infirmities of the weak; it struggles in discomfort for the sake of helping another person discover peace.

Don't worry if it does not happen to you overnight. Remember, I have lived through so many storms that I can grade them now. I give them classifications and categories. The key is to use your inner strength to survive them and then proceed to the next level of thriving past them. I have one last tip to help you do this.

Look around you. Look on your social media feed, look at the evening news, reach out to a family member, or check on old friends and pay attention to what you hear. There is always someone going through adversity worse than yours. You may have a college classmate battling a drug or alcohol addiction. You may have a coworker who lost a spouse in a drunk driving accident or know a neighbor who is burying their only son or daughter killed in the line of duty in active military service. You may have a cousin who is happily married but is fighting bouts of depression because she and her husband have just miscarried their first child. If you look for someone to encourage during your storm, you will always see the light faster.

Storm Playbook Study

Chapter Summary

- The aftermath of a storm can provide a path for new opportunities and developments.
- During the post-storm rebuilding process, undiscovered talents and strengths can be discovered and implemented.
- The ability to recognize and uncover hidden strengths requires the development of a keen spiritual eye; unlocking the revelation power to gain insight beyond your natural eyesight is key.
- The storm's aftermath presents each individual with a figurative two-way mirror that allows you to see who you were before the storm and who you are becoming after it passes. The post-storm period also allows each person to assess their strengths and weaknesses.

Journaling

1. Have you discovered new strengths in the aftermath of your storm? What are they, and how will you continue to develop them?
2. Who in your circle of influence needs support and encouragement right now? Which lessons have you learned that would benefit them?

Storm Survivor: Noah

Vacation Bible School and Sunday school are not as prominent in modern churches as they were back in the day. These are supplemental Bible studies—the first happening for one week annually in the summer and the latter usually occurring before Sunday morning church services. One of the most popular Bible stories studied in these sessions is Noah and the ark. Often the students reenact the story for maximum impact. Bible teachers are not the only ones who thought the story would make a good script. The movies *Evan Almighty* and *Noah* are both Noah-themed stories. I will not tell you my opinion of the motion pictures, but what I will say is that the biblical story of Noah is definitely big-screen worthy.

God decided that the human race needed a do-over, and He selected Noah and his family to create a new beginning for humanity. Noah faced some pretty serious ridicule from his neighbors, considering it had never rained before. If social media were around back then, the new memes about him would have been endless! Nevertheless, Noah was obedient, and God used him to repopulate the earth.

> Then God said to Noah and to his sons with him: "I now establish my covenant with you and with your descendants after you and with every living creature that was with you—the birds, the livestock and all the wild animals, all those that came out of the ark with you—every living creature on earth. I establish my covenant with you: Never again will all life be destroyed by the waters of a flood; never again will there be a flood to destroy the earth."

And God said, "This is the sign of the covenant I am making between me and you and every living creature with you, a covenant for all generations to come: I have set my rainbow in the clouds, and it will be the sign of the covenant between me and the earth. Whenever I bring clouds over the earth and the rainbow appears in the clouds, I will remember my covenant between me and you and all living creatures of every kind. Never again will the waters become a flood to destroy all life." (Gen. 9:8–15)

Storm Song

Noah's story reminds me of another song that you should add to your Storm Song playlist: "Moving Forward" by Israel Houghton.

Memory Verse

"Forget the former things;
do not dwell on the past.
See, I am doing a new thing!
Now it springs up; do you not perceive it?
I am making a way in the wilderness
and streams in the wasteland."

—Isaiah 43:18–19

CHAPTER 5

Compartmentalizing the Impact

When you face a crisis of any kind, it is imperative that you first have a scale by which to measure the gravity of the experience, but after that, you need to understand how to compartmentalize the impact. Compartmentalization is a coping strategy to help you deal with everyday life. To utilize this strategy effectively, you must know what your core values are.

Our culture today is filled with topics that cause disagreement. One of the best ways to handle the constant tension is to compartmentalize. Today's millennials (and Generation Z) are often very uncomfortable when older African Americans discuss race relations. Until the recently publicized incidents of police brutality, many younger people felt that racism was something of the past. The experiences of older African Americans who grew up during segregation and even integration were often unfathomable to them. They just did not have a category for that level of racism. But when that same younger generation began to see people of color being murdered by police officers, seemingly unjustly in most cases, they were shaken to the core, suddenly struck by awareness of the stigma and historical remnants of the consequences of being a person of color in America. It became essential to compartmentalize the impact of the situation and focus on strategies to improve the present conditions.

Dealing with the aftermath of a storm requires this same level of compartmentalization. After you have cried and grieved over your loss, you must shift your mind-set to begin to give that suffering meaning. Once you can identify what happened to you and how it affected you, you are now ready to assess how to process it—how all the layers of the challenge have changed or altered various areas of your life. After this process is complete, you are ready to move toward your purpose; you now know who you are.

Another area in which compartmentalization is important is the #MeToo movement, which picked up steam after actress Alyssa Milano encouraged women to speak out by tweeting their experiences with sexual harassment and assault with the hashtag #MeToo. The #MeToo movement often cites Alyssa Milano as the movement's founder; however, the original sentiment was birthed by a black woman ten years earlier. Should African American women be outraged that it took a white celebrity female voice to restart the conversation? I don't think so. I think the important thing is that a woman (regardless of who she was) used a social media platform that was not available a decade previously to empower women around the globe and create an environment of justice and healing. The movement was so profound that the original African American #MeToo founder, Tarana Burke, was featured with other brave "silence-breaking" women on the 2017 *Time* Person of the Year cover.

The movement led to exposure of mistreatment and harassment in Hollywood that had been going on in unimaginable ways. While I am encouraged by the victories of these women (and men) who have come forward and shared their stories, I think about the decades that these women and men suffered in silence. This type of compartmentalization is not beneficial; I encourage you never to compartmentalize something to the point it causes you harm. You should never allow yourself to be abused or mistreated for any reason. We cannot change the past, but we can heal ourselves by controlling our present and our future.

I am glad that women have finally had enough. I am excited to see that women are organizing marches and fighting for their rights. I am excited that children have had enough of school violence and are standing up for themselves. I am encouraged that athletes are taking a stand against police brutality. I think these examples are relevant because sometimes you must compartmentalize long enough to devise a strategy to get out of the storm, and other times you have to compartmentalize to survive the storm.

There is a method to the madness. Compartmentalization, when appropriately used, is a tool that allows the mind to deal with conflicting internal emotions simultaneously. I want to give you healthy ways to use this coping tool.

First, create categories for your values and prioritize them. I will use my categories as an example:

1. Relationship with God
2. Relationship with my husband
3. My immediate family relationships
4. My churches and ministry responsibilities
5. Time for myself
6. Community activities
7. Legacy and succession planning
8. Celebrations and recreation

Almost everything important in my life is compartmentalized into one of these categories. Knowing how my life is made up shows me where to place other matters as they arise. When Hurricane Katrina hit our lives, I had very little time for myself or recreation. I certainly wasn't thinking about legacy and succession; I was focused on the immediate situation. But amid rebuilding, my husband's gift of organization kicked in, and my gifts of help and creativity came back to life.

In a storm, you must not allow yourself to drown in emotions but instead let God touch your spirit within so you can do what you are called to do at that time. After Katrina, it was important that we as pastors gave our church family direction and a sense of normalcy, but it was also important that each of our children felt safe and secure in the truth that life was changing but not ending. My baby girl was a senior in high school and was snatched from her normal routine during that important time. My eldest daughter had already experienced the tragedy of losing her first and only child, and then she lost her home and all her belongings. My son, PJ, was in college in Atlanta and was worried about his family. He met us when we got to Georgia and was relieved to know we had survived the storm. Thank God we didn't just survive, we began to thrive.

I needed to prioritize and pay attention. Yes, I was a preacher, but I also needed to be a mother at that time. I did normal things with them, like eating breakfast, lunch, and dinner together. We had TV nights as well, and I let them talk and talk and talk so I could gauge where they were psychologically and spiritually. We did not have a church home at the time, but that was okay because our family was and is our first ministry. We worshipped and prayed at home.

Once my family felt secure, I shifted back to my work as co-pastor and resumed all the ministerial tasks of running the church. I had to make a concerted effort to prevent my immediate situation from making me abandon the values I had deemed important to my overall happiness and well-being before the tragedy of Katrina. Too often we allow tragic events to make us feel that our previously established values aren't worth fighting for anymore. Thankfully, compartmentalizing allows us to handle a situation at face value without abandoning our core values. My kids repeatedly asked me about the new home we'd just bought and about other things we'd lost. I responded each time, "Are you kidding me? After losing Kai, my first grandbaby, as long as I have you guys with me, I'm happy!"

I know many parents who have to compartmentalize so that they can still fulfill their parental duties. For example, I know a lady whose teenage daughter had been suspended from school for truancy and disrespecting school officials. Even though the mother had taught her daughter the importance of education and respect for authority, her child violated her trust. When that same mother received a phone call that her child had suffered an injury and needed immediate care, she dropped everything and went to her daughter. While respect for authority and education are important values to her, the overall health and well-being of her daughter were more critical in that moment, so she focused on attending to those needs. The mother didn't abandon her values. She chose to compartmentalize them for the sake of her child. She had to calm down, think, then move in wisdom and not mere emotion.

Take a moment to determine what your core values are. Now that you know your categories, you can use compartmentalization strategies to ensure that you are functioning optimally through your challenge. Your implementation requires a few things:

1. Focus on the things that matter the most.
2. Become disciplined about setting and maintaining a schedule.
3. Understand your triggers. Be completely aware of the types of situations most likely to throw you off course.
4. Use a calendar. Schedule everything, even time with your family. It will help you stay on task and minimize stress.
5. Breathe/take a break. Remember the necessity of taking time throughout your day to take a mental break, even if it's for only fifteen to thirty minutes.
6. Eat regularly. You will be surprised how eating at regularly scheduled intervals increases your energy and productivity.

Now that you understand the importance of categorizing your values, we can discuss how you can minimize the impact of the storm.

———

First, you admit the level of devastation that has occurred in your life. You cannot conquer it until you confront it. Denial is never the answer when dealing with a storm. Next, you must accept the changes that have occurred because of the crisis. Then you must decide to create a life that feeds your faith instead of your fear. It is easy to live in a state of perpetual fear when you survive a tragedy. Don't accept that destructive lifestyle. Fear is

False
Evidence
Acting
Real

The evil forces in life will follow behind you, whispering, "It's going to happen again!" You should respond back, "Not if I can help it!" We must take control of our destiny from the enemy. You must not give in to the overwhelming urge to have a pity party for yourself. I suggest you find an anti–pity party partner to help you remain accountable in this area. It may be a parent, spouse, friend, or sibling, but I suggest that you find someone who will let you vent and then encourage you to get up and keep going.

Finally, do not be afraid to get help from mentors or counselors with this process. Some of us were raised by parents who had unhealthy coping skills. It is often difficult to operate against your genetics and your environmental upbringing. Sometimes you need a mentor or professional who is well versed in that area to help you. Sometimes you may need a pastor who can guide you from a spiritual perspective. As a pastor, I want to say that not every issue is spiritual. Instead, you may be battling a soul issue that requires a psychologist to help you.

The soul is the place where your emotional and mental health reside. There are experiences that can damage an individual's capacity to love, trust, and be confident. For example, experiencing violence, sexual assault, heartbreak, or any type of abuse or addiction can cause soul issues, which require counseling. Because of so much abuse and negative experiences occurring in our world, I believe that churches need to offer counseling services within a spiritual context, as that will lead to faster recovery. Then deliverance will happen in the body, spirit, *and* soul.

This is important because often when we are violated in some way, the pain is so great we bury it. The problem with burying pain is that it always resurfaces, so it is better to deal with it up front. If you are a survivor like the brave individuals who have come forward as a result of the #MeToo movement, counseling can help you heal from that situation. If you find a trustworthy, qualified person to help you, the impact of the challenge will lessen as you are healed.

Storm Playbook Study

Chapter Summary

- Compartmentalization can be an effective coping mechanism.
- When used appropriately, this invaluable coping tool assists the mind in dealing with conflicting internal emotions simultaneously.
- Two areas where compartmentalization is often essential:
  ◦ Relationship with God
  ◦ Relationships with others (spouse/family members/ friends/coworkers)
- Compartmentalization helps individuals face challenges more pragmatically and calmly.
- Compartmentalization allows individuals to face situations in ways that prevent them from compromising their core values.

Journaling

1. Make a list of your values and prioritize them. Then determine where the effects of your current storm fit into your list.
2. Identify outside resources (such as pastors, counselors,

psychologists) who can help you, or others, cope with the storms you are facing.

Storm Survivor: The Syrophoenician Woman

Sometimes our greatest challenges arise from misunderstandings from people we believe are there to help us. This next storm survivor was so focused on receiving what she needed, she did not allow offense or hurt feelings to sidetrack her.

> And going away from there, Jesus withdrew to the district of Tyre and Sidon.
>
> And behold, a woman who was a Canaanite from that district came out and, with a [loud, troublesomely urgent] cry, begged, Have mercy on me, O Lord, Son of David! My daughter is miserably and distressingly and cruelly possessed by a demon!
>
> But He did not answer her a word. And His disciples came and implored Him, saying, Send her away, for she is crying out after us.
>
> He answered, I was sent only to the lost sheep of the house of Israel.
>
> But she came and, kneeling, worshiped Him and kept praying, Lord, help me!
>
> And He answered, It is not right (proper, becoming, or fair) to take the children's bread and throw it to the little dogs.
>
> She said, Yes, Lord, yet even the little pups (little whelps) eat the crumbs that fall from their [young] masters' table.
>
> Then Jesus answered her, O woman, great is your faith! Be it done for you as you wish. And her daughter was cured from that moment. (Matt. 15:21–28 AMPC)

If you did not read it for yourself, you might not believe this story is actually in the Bible. I have read it in several different translations because I had to be sure I had read it correctly before I started telling people that Jesus referred to healing this women's child in the same conversation that He mentioned throwing bread to dogs. As troubling as these words may seem, the thing I love about this woman is that she was so focused on receiving what she needed from Jesus that she compartmentalized whatever she might have felt about the metaphor and proceeded to request what she needed. Jesus then granted her request because of her faith. The Syrophoenician woman is a great example of compartmentalizing emotional distress to get to a breakthrough. I have often counseled men and women who were so close to receiving their blessing from the Lord but had grown weary.

I encourage you to be faithful at work, even if you have an unfair boss. I encourage you to keep praying for the teen or adult child who has lost their way. Always remember that the effectual fervent prayers of the righteous avail much, and even when God does not show up according to our timing, He always shows up on time.

Memory Verse

Humble yourselves, therefore, under God's mighty hand, that he may lift you up in due time. Cast all your anxiety on him because he cares for you.

—1 Peter 5:6–7

CHAPTER 6
Holding On to Hope

Inspiration is a source of hope, and hope is a crucial component of the Storm Playbook. Many of the most inspirational stories and movies of all time are based (at least in part) on actual events.

The 2016 movie *Miracles from Heaven* is an excellent example of art imitating life. If you are not familiar with it, I highly recommend you see it. It is based on the incredible true story of the Beam family from Burleson, Texas. Their ten-year-old daughter, Anna, was diagnosed with an incurable digestive motility disorder that threatened her life, which ultimately tested the entire family's faith. Just when it seemed all hope was lost, Anna was playing with her sister, climbing a tree, when the tree branch cracked and Anna fell thirty feet down a hole in the tree.

After her fall, the paramedics and the press showed up on the scene. During all the turmoil, her mother, Christy, broke down and started to pray. The medics were able to rescue Anna out of the tree. At the hospital, the doctor said that other than a mild concussion from the fall, Anna was okay.

Later Anna told her parents that when she hit her head after the fall, everything went black and she had an out-of-body experience. She saw a butterfly and touched it, which brought her to heaven. In the movie, Anna walks through colorful woods before approaching the gates of heaven. She says she spoke to God, and while she wanted to stay, He told her she must return and that she would be healed. Anna says she knows people probably wouldn't believe her story, but later in the movie she boldly shares her story with others in small groups and gatherings, despite the skepticism of many in the crowd.

The movie ends with a scene of the Beams having a pizza dinner, showing that Anna is all better. Side note: I love movies with happy endings, but that is not why I recommend it. I shared it with you to show you that in both art and life there is power in inspirational stories. Therefore, if you are struggling with hopelessness, I recommend you go on a quest to discover things that ignite the flames of hope within you!

If you think about it, hope can be found in several places. If you attend church regularly, you may experience hope through a sermon or Bible story. If you frequent social networking channels (as most of us do), you may follow people who give you hope through quotes, short videos, and personal testimonials. If you are an avid TV viewer, you may have a few TV shows that stir up your faith and help you overcome your fears. For instance, if you're struggling with the challenge of weight loss, the show *The Biggest Loser* can serve as a vehicle of motivation, and that motivation may increase your hope and belief that you can reach your desired weight-loss goal. For others, it may be a best friend, family member, or significant other who always provides the stimulus needed to view the glass half-full instead of half-empty.

Regardless of what your source of hope may be, it is imperative that you find it and hold on to it. Proverbs 13:12 says, "Hope deferred makes the heart sick, but when the desire comes, it is a tree of life" (NKJV).

I like how the *Benson's Commentary* explains the meaning of hope deferred: "The delay of that which a man eagerly desires and expects is such an affliction that it differs little from a lingering disease." It further explains the second half of the verse: "When the good desired and expected is obtained. *It is a tree of life*—That is, most sweet, satisfactory, and reviving to the soul."[1]

This verse emphasizes the importance of holding on to your hope. In Greek, the word "hope" is *elpis*, which can be translated as "the expectation of good."[2] There is power in expecting things to get better. Typically there is some activity or action that is required on your part to transform your situation, but sometimes the first step to life getting better is believing that it can.

As a religious leader, I have been counseling people for decades. I have seen couples with horrible relationships turn their marriages around because they came together and agreed that they wanted the relationship to get better and wholeheartedly believed it was possible. At the same time, I have seen couples whose relationships were not in dire shape quit because one or both people had no hope it would improve. Those couples almost always ended up divorcing or, worse, staying together in a dysfunctional and toxic relationship. In fact, during and after Katrina, many couples I knew broke up. Strangely, some could not find their mate, but I later discovered these couples' marriages had already been on the rocks; the storm just took them out. Hope was already gone for one or both partners. The wind of the storm was all that was needed to blow them apart.

The pressure of tragedy can make or break you. So it is imperative to maintain your hope, for hope will increase your faith.

Hope is confidence that the situation will work. During difficult times, I choose to believe that my circumstances are working out for my good. Then my hope transforms into faith. My faith says, "I know it can work!" That faith is produced from the foundation of your hope. My hope is magnified and inspired by my faith and connection to God in the Spirit and the Scriptures. Scriptures I find encouraging include Romans 5:3–5 and Romans 8:28, "And we know that all things work together for good" (NKJV). Hope matters.

The first step in having a better life, job, or relationship is believing that it is possible. The next step is acknowledging the work that will be required to achieve that desired outcome.

———

Many times you have to hope against hope; you'll need to keep believing that things will improve, even when the likelihood is slim. That may sound strange, but you will face times when nothing around you says that things will work out. That's when faith must kick in. Faith is not what you can see; it's what you believe.

There is a story in the Bible I love about a woman who had been sick (bleeding) for twelve long years. She had spent all her money on doctors and medicine, but they did not cure her. However, she heard that Jesus, who had healed many, was in town. She went to see Him, but the crowd was thick. I assume it would be difficult for her, being weak and a woman, to get through the multitude. She said to herself, "If I may touch but his clothes, I shall be whole." I interpret that to mean, "Even if He doesn't see me, if I touch His hem, I will be healed." I believe that hope within her gave her the strength to push through. When she got close to Him, she touched His hem and strength came into her body. Jesus instantly knew that someone had touched Him because He felt virtue leave His body (Mark 5:25–30 KJV). Whether you are a believer or not, this is a fantastic story because it shows what hope can do. People, sicknesses, and other circumstances seem to respond to our words and thoughts of hope and faith.

I have a personal story to share that supports this principle. When I was halfway through my pregnancy with my third child, I was taking a bath when suddenly the tub began to fill with blood. I gasped, thinking we had lost our baby. I immediately went to see my doctor, who began watching the baby's blood count. He told me that if it dropped to a certain number, we would have to abort. Though a little afraid, I decided I wanted that baby. I knew God had a purpose for her because of the spiritual attacks I had faced while carrying her.

I began to speak these words over my baby: "Health and wholeness, in Jesus' name!" The blood count number remained good, and all was well until I went into labor. At the hospital, as I was waiting for the labor pains to increase, my husband left to get a bite to eat. While he was gone, the attending nurse (I loved her) noticed the umbilical cord had wrapped around my baby's neck. When she saw it on the monitor, she called my doctor to do an emergency C-section, which I had not experienced before. I asked if we could wait for my hubby to return, but the nurse said there wasn't time. We needed to rush and get that baby out of harm's way.

I began to repeat those words again and put them in the atmosphere all around me. I wanted the environment, the nurse, the doctor, my hubby, and the evil one to know what my hope was. My husband and the nurse agreed with me. I repeatedly said, "Health and wholeness, in Jesus' name!" My hope did not make me ashamed. My little Christiann Xani (An-nee) Morton was born a beautiful, healthy baby girl. I made up a song from that experience. Even now, we sometimes sing it together:

Christiann Xani,
So sweet to me!
I put Christ in her name,
so whenever the evil one tries to mess with her,
he will see in whom she and her mommy's faith and hope rest.

Hope it! Believe it! Now speak it! After you believe that something positive can happen, and after you understand and commit to an action plan, you are on your way to overcoming your present hardship.

Strategies to Keep Your Hope Alive

1. Change your mind-set.

If you are going to hold on to your hope, you first have to win the battle in your mind. You must change your mind-set so that you remain hopeful in the midst of seemingly hopeless situations. The following strategies will help:

Be determined to learn from the past.

Bestselling author John C. Maxwell wrote a book titled *Sometimes You Win—Sometimes You Learn*. The entire premise of the book is about learning lessons from loss and challenge. I encourage you to do that with every failure you face. Take some time and look at what you learned from the situation. Focusing on what you learned will help you look at the loss in a more positive way and help keep you from repeating a mistake.

Focus on the future.

No matter how bad the situation is right now, you are still alive. If you have breath in your lungs, there is still more for you to do on earth. Every day we learn of people we know and don't know who have passed away. Some die from accidents, some from sickness, and others from natural causes, but regardless of the reason, they are no longer here. That is not the case with you or me. So roll up your sleeves and get to work. Each of us has a God-ordained purpose. We were created with a unique assignment to be fulfilled.

Maximize the present.

Sometimes you need to put your phone down, shut off your computer, and fully immerse yourself in the here and now. There are moments in our lives we miss because we are busy beating ourselves up over past mistakes or we are too focused on our five-, ten-, or fifteen-year plan. Planning for the future is vital, but be careful not to be so focused on what's next that you miss what's going on right now. I know many successful people who would trade all their money to go back and spend more time with a family member they had neglected while building their empire. I am not saying that success is bad, but I am saying it is critical to learn how to balance your career and business aspirations while prioritizing your relationships.

Your marriage will not survive forever on autopilot. Your children will not be young forever—there are some values you must teach them while they are young. Your parents will not live forever—you must schedule the time to spend with them. Often I have found that among the individuals who grieve the hardest are those who lost a loved one they did not spend much time with because they always thought they would have more time. I recently read a quote from Bishop Rosie O'neal that said, "Procrastination is the arrogant assumption that God owes you another chance to do tomorrow what He gave you the chance to do today." Now, that packs a powerful punch. We should never assume that we will have another chance. We must make the most of every opportunity, seize the day, and maximize the present.

2. Eliminate negativity from your life.

One way you can keep your hope alive is by making a good confession, declaration, or affirmation over your life and circumstances. Speaking positively over your life is often easier said than done, because we are all bombarded by negativity constantly. There are four ways I cut negativity from my life on a regular basis.

Eliminate toxic, draining people.

I love people. I am a pastor. I am in the "people business." But I learned a long time ago that there are some people I can't afford to spend significant time with because their negativity is contagious. If you have ever been having a good day and got a call from someone (a relative, colleague, or friend) and after talking to them you felt worse, then you know precisely what I mean.

I am not talking about someone who is calling you to vent or someone who is simply having a bad day. I mean someone who is always sad and negative. If you know someone like this, I am not saying that you should never talk to them. Often they are people in your life whom you must talk to, so I am just saying you must limit their access to you or the amount of time that you spend together. For example, if it is a parent, you may choose to talk to them for the last ten minutes of your commute to work so that the conversation will have a definite ending time. I know it may sound extreme, but you will be surprised how much easier it is to hold on to your hope when the drain is not constantly being unplugged from your figurative hope "sink."

Extract yourself from negative situations.

When you are fighting to maintain hope in your life, there are some situations you should avoid. I have found that when we are living our best lives, it is easier to believe the best. To me, "living your best life" happens when we are walking in our individual purposes and are avoiding situations that create negative emotions or action. If we focus on thinking right, talking right, and living right, we will find that it is easier to hold on to hope.

Stop focusing on people's negative opinion of you or your past.

Decide to divorce yourself from others' opinion of you. The truth is that there are some people who will always look at you through a negative lens. As long as you are living your best life and being the absolute best version of yourself that you can be, you can't let their opinion affect you.

Make a good confession.

Words have power. If you have spent any significant time in church, you have probably heard the verse "Death and life are in the power of the tongue," found in Proverbs 18:21 (NKJV). One way to keep your hope alive is by speaking hope over your life daily. So, right now, I want you to do an exercise with me. Fill in the blanks below:

I am a conqueror. I am victorious.
I am_____.
Although I have suffered greatly, today is a new day and
I know that my best days are yet to come. I will work
diligently until _____happens.
I know that I will be successful because
_____and_____.
I know that gratitude is important and I am grateful for
_____.
I will never give up because _____.
Every day I chose to win because defeat is not an option.

I want you to read the confession out loud every day for twenty-one days, because anything you do for twenty-one days becomes a habit. If you make speaking positivity into your life a practice, it will change your outlook and give you hope. If this affirmation doesn't quite fit for you, then use mine as a formula for writing your own. It's just important that you do it.

3. Guard your time.

There is nothing that will affect your mind-set like wasted time. Be determined and strategic about whom you spend time with and what you spend time doing. Billionaire Warren Buffett said, "The difference between successful people and very successful people is that very successful people say no to almost everything."[3] Increased success will increase your hope.

If you adopt these strategies in your life, you will find that it is a lot easier to keep your hope buckets filled!

Storm Playbook Study

Chapter Summary

- Hope is one of the most vital components of your Storm Playbook.
- Seek hope in your daily/weekly activities, such as:
  - Attending worship and sermons during church services or viewing via media platforms
  - Reading and viewing positive social media accounts/ channels
  - Fellowshipping with other positive people in your life
- Implement hope strategies:
  - Shift your mind-set.
  - Focus on the future while maximizing the present.
  - Eliminate negative people from your life, or at least your inner circle.
  - Extract yourself from negative and toxic situations as soon as you can.
  - Your words have power. Make sure to consistently and continually speak life and not death over your life and the lives of others; make a good confession!

Journaling

1. What activities do you currently use to find hope? What activities can you add after reading this chapter?
2. What ways will you deliberately and intentionally focus on the future while maximizing your present?
3. What is one hope strategy you learned that you would like to share with someone else? Who is it?

Storm Survivor: The Shunammite Woman

The Shunammite woman is a dual storm survivor.

First, the Shunammite woman survived infertility (2 Kings 4:14). She reminds me of women I know who have waited on a desire of their heart for so long, they have quietly given up. These women are not bitter or angry. Quite the opposite. They serve in multiple areas of ministry and are faithful volunteers; however, there is something they long for more than anything else. They just keep moving so that the sting of the absence of "that one thing" does not paralyze them.

The Shunammite woman was a blessing to the prophet Elisha. In a present-day church, she might have been a lead greeter, the leader of the hospitality ministry, or a member of the pastoral care team. Elisha was determined to grant the secret petition of her heart, and only a year after his prophesying that she would have the child she had been longing for, she gave birth to a son (vv. 15–17). But after the child grew older, the unthinkable happened. Her son got a terrible headache and died (vv. 18–20).

This woman could have simply thanked God for the time that she had been allowed to be the boy's mother and buried her son, but this mother held on to hope that her son could be healed. So she took him back to the person who started the miracle in the first place and challenged him. She put a demand on Elisha's anointing to bring her baby back to life by the power of the almighty God, and that is just what happened.

> When she reached the man of God at the mountain, she took hold of his feet. Gehazi came over to push her away, but the man of God said, "Leave her alone! She is in bitter distress, but the LORD has hidden it from me and has not told me why."
>
> "Did I ask you for a son, my lord?" she said. "Didn't I tell you, 'Don't raise my hopes'?" . . .
>
> When Elisha reached the house, there was the boy lying dead on his couch. He went in, shut the door on the two of them and prayed to the LORD. Then he got on the bed and lay on the boy, mouth to mouth, eyes to eyes, hands to hands. As he stretched himself out on him, the boy's body grew warm. Elisha turned away and walked back and forth in the room and then got on the bed and stretched out on him once more. The boy sneezed seven times and opened his eyes.
>
> Elisha summoned Gehazi and said, "Call the Shunammite." And he did. When she came, he said, "Take your son." She came in, fell at his feet and bowed to the ground. Then she took her son and went out. (vv. 27–28, 32–37)

Never underestimate the power of your hope and faith to completely resurrect a dead situation in your life and help you restore life after the storm.

Memory Verse

Let us hold unswervingly to the hope we profess, for he who promised is faithful.

—Hebrews 10:23

CHAPTER 7

Insight Beyond Eyesight

I recently discovered a book by Harvard-trained researcher Shawn Achor titled *Before Happiness*. The basic premise of the book is that happiness is a necessary precursor to success. In the book, Achor hesitantly admits that even though he is a Harvard guy, he must praise one thing that is done right at Yale: all first-year medical students are required to take an art class. He explains that the class teaches the importance of perspective and considering different vantage points. After the medical students are taught how to look for detail in centuries-old paintings, the students then attempt to diagnose health issues for their patients. As a result of cross-training their brains, they increase their ability to detect critical medical details by an astonishing 10 percent. He adds that multiple vantage points multiply the opportunities for successful actions.[1] Achor's observation is a perfect example of perspective. The medical students were introduced to something new that expanded their ability to see and interpret data beyond the limitations they had before their exposure to the art class.

Perspective is everything. When your world is falling apart, what you choose to focus on is critical. I encourage you to pay attention to the details of your particular situation.

To commit to our unique purpose, we must be careful not to overly concern ourselves with another person's purpose. Yes, we can care, especially when it comes to family and friends, but we cannot overdo it. When I watch the reality show *The Real Housewives* and others like it, everyone in the show seems to be more concerned about other people's lives than their own. Much of the bickering and fights we see are caused by people being overly concerned about another's purpose.

Of course, those shows reflect real life. They teach us that we must be careful not to let our concern for someone else become an obsession that we secretly use to fulfill something lacking in our own lives. If we have become envious and jealous of other people, then we probably need to examine ourselves. If this is true, we must not deny it. There are reasons for those feelings. We must evaluate our self-worth and self-esteem. We must internally find out where the feelings started and why we value others more than we value ourselves. Self-evaluation can lead you to a painful place, but I believe looking for truth is a brave thing to do. It defeats the lies you have told yourself for years and empowers you to start with a clean slate.

Often your most significant source of pain is the key to unlocking your most significant power. I once heard of a woman who travels all over the world and rescues women who are victims of sex trafficking. As a former trafficking victim herself, she decided to dedicate her entire life to saving others. Now, she could have let that devastating experience hold her captive and keep her lost in its misery, but she didn't. She refused to let her experience make her bitter; instead, she decided to make the lives of others better. During Hurricane Katrina and the disasters that have followed, I've heard many stories from victims who were moved to help others although they were suffering themselves.

I love a book that one of my church members wrote called *I Prayed Through the Storm*. As she chronicled her experience day by day—even the horror of being in the Superdome during and following Hurricane Katrina—she highlighted those who were helpful. She had never written a book before, but her perspective produced her first published work.

Another example of how one's perspective can create success is my spiritual daughter who is in the armed forces. More than once she has shared with me the trauma she experienced when she was at war. Once she returned to the States, she found it difficult for a while waiting for life to return to normal. Yet in that process she became sensitive to military parents who have to leave their children when they are on a tour of duty, so she opened a day care on a military base. She loves and takes exceptional care of those children. She even uses FaceTime to video chat with parents during the children's activities so they don't have to miss special moments. I am so moved by her thoughtfulness.

Remembering and using helpful coping strategies bring people hope more quickly. These strategies are often the difference between surviving a tough experience so that you can thrive afterward or allowing it to drive you crazy. There are several beneficial strategies:

- **Adaptive mechanisms:** those that offer real help
- **Behavioral mechanisms:** those that change what we do
- **Cognitive mechanisms:** those that change what we think
- **Conversion mechanisms:** those that change one thing into another

There are also harmful strategies to avoid:

- **Attack mechanisms:** those that push discomfort onto others
- **Avoidance mechanisms:** those that avoid the issue
- **Defense mechanisms:** those that you use to defend yourself. There are many of them, but two of the most common are displacement and projection.
- **Self-harm mechanisms:** those that hurt us when we use them

We will not deal with all of the above mechanisms in this chapter, but I want to highlight a few for you. The first one, the adaptive mechanism, is what the young woman who rescues victims of sex trafficking used. She further tapped into a subcategory of the adaptive mechanism of posttraumatic growth, which is defined as using the energy of trauma for good. This mechanism is often employed by women who survive domestic abuse, take time to heal, and grow from their pain by helping others in abusive relationships. Some do it by volunteering at women's shelters, while others may donate money to domestic abuse charities. In both cases, the survivors have a healthy perspective about overcoming their experience and see the need to give back.

Some of the mechanisms are not positive at all. Have you ever heard the phrase, "Hurting people hurt people"? Sometimes people who are suffering lash out and hurt others. This is known as the attack mechanism. It also has several subcategories:

- **Displacement:** the shifting of intended action to a safer target
- **Fight-or-flight reaction:** reacting by attacking or running away

- **Passive aggression:** refusal by passive avoidance
- **Projection:** seeing the individual's unwanted feelings in other people
- **Trivializing:** making something small that is actually big

I wanted to share these with you for a couple of reasons. First, so you will know when you are being attacked. Second, so you can recognize if you are attacking someone else. It is always much better if we can identify faults within ourselves and self-correct. Perspective helps you heal from your storm and prevents you from adopting negative coping mechanisms as a result of unresolved issues and pain.

The Power of Perspective

How can you increase the positivity of your perspective on difficulties and trials?

1. Change your overall life perspective.

See your life as a marathon and not a sprint. A sprint is very different from a marathon. A sprint covers a short distance and lasts just a few seconds, while a marathon covers miles and lasts for hours. A sprinter must be prepared to exert all their energy instantly, while a marathon runner must carefully measure out their energy to endure to the end of the race.

2. Commit to your purpose.

There is power in embracing your purpose. You do things differently based on working toward your individual goals. Sometimes success eludes us because we set ourselves up for failure. I say "we" because I have been guilty of this as well. It is easy to look at commercials or social media feeds and want someone else's gift or life. The reality is that your purest form of success will be obtained only through embracing your unique gift and calling. Although my husband and I are pastors, our only son, PJ Morton, is a super-talented neo-soul singer and producer. I am biased because I am his mother, but he is also a two-time Grammy-nominated artist and performs for sold-out shows all over the world.

There is power in accepting who you are and using your gifts. If you do this and stay in your own lane, you will reap an entirely different level of success. My son told me he wanted to be himself and blaze a new trail, demonstrating that Christians can be multi-faceted. A Morehouse graduate, he became a leader and developer of other musicians. His career has taken him around the world, inspiring thousands within and outside the church. Pastors' kids live in glass houses and are sometimes judged rather harshly; it can stifle or destroy them. I'm grateful that he and my other two children found strength from insight rather than eyesight.

3. Stop waiting for the perfect time.

Perfection is the enemy of successful action. You must start. There will never be a perfect situation, so you must begin with what you have and be determined to build on that foundation a little more each day. Of course, you do have to use wisdom. I am not encouraging you to hurry into something crazy! I am explicitly talking about stalling unnecessarily.

We've heard that time waits for no one, but more than that, at a certain age you may look back and see time has left you with some dreams that will never come true because the seasons have changed. Knowing that a season will not return without a miracle because the circumstances are different is a terrible feeling. To avoid experiencing this feeling of regret, make sure you are sensitive to life's weather changes. Don't wait until the sun is shining; sometimes you've got to move in the rain. After Katrina, the storm was still raging, but we had to see beyond the storm. After about a month of helping everyone else feel secure, we had to ask God, "What's next?" He led us forward, putting us back on the path to purposeful and fruitful ministry. My advice is, rain or shine, keep moving.

A biblical example of this is when Peter heard Jesus' voice as He walked on the water. As Jesus got closer, Peter barely could see Him but was willing to trust Him; he asked Jesus to allow him to walk toward Him on the water (Matt. 14:22–33). The lesson I receive from this story is that my faith must not only be *in* something but *toward* something, whatever that something is. We must be willing to go after it even though we can't see where we are going. In the midst of uncertainty, we must keep our focus lest we begin to sink in fear. As the winds started to blow, Peter became afraid and began to sink, but Jesus caught him (vv. 30–31).

Peter had courage to get out of the boat, but not enough to keep walking. Friends, storms come with wind and rain. Success does not come without its challenges, but just know—if you're being led by your inner-sight to go forward, keep walking. You may get wet, but the waters will not overtake you.

4. Get the help you need to succeed.

Sometimes we fail because we lack one of the ingredients for our success. That missing ingredient can be a person who has a skill you don't possess. The missing element might be the knowledge you need to obtain, whether by continuing your education, receiving a certification, or simply reading a relevant book. Know that you don't have to have all the answers yourself.

———

Pia Silva is a successful author and businesswoman. During an interview, she told the story of how one significant tweak in her business model was a game changer for the business she owns with her husband.[2] Their "secret sauce" involved changing the method in which they brand their clients, which eliminated almost all their overhead. This one change in their deliverables allowed them to serve their clients better, make more money, and do it all in less time. Silva calls it the 50/25/25 Formula to Profit and Freedom, which means spending 50 percent of your time working for paying clients, 25 percent building your brand and enhancing your value (through training/seminars/classes), and the last 25 percent on leisure or meaningful activities (basically anything except working).[3] If you are a business owner, you may not need an MBA; the answer for you may be found in the pages of a book written by another business owner.

This area can be challenging if we don't want to admit that we don't have the answers. But you may be just one person away from success. Smart managers and CEOs staff their weaknesses. If everyone you hire is exactly like you, success may evade you; good teams work because everyone has a position. Sports provide a great example of this. How effective would a basketball team be if every player was a guard? A mix of talent and teamwork wins games.

Your perception fine-tunes your vision. Your ability to see the details that matter, and push past the ones that don't, is pivotal when you are navigating beyond a storm season. Your perception also fuels faith and banishes fear.

Faith is an essential perspective for success after a storm. Now, I realize *faith* may seem like a religious or spiritual word to you if you aren't a frequent churchgoer, but I assure you, you use faith every day. If you ride public transportation or even use an Uber, you are using faith because you depend on someone you do not know to take you to your destination safely. In most instances, you do not know anything about your driver. You don't know if they are a functioning alcoholic or a drug addict. You don't know if they have some disorder that is controlled by medications. You don't know. You must have a blind trust that the person operating the vehicle will get you to your destination safely.

Unfortunately, we live in a time that requires faith to send your children to school. The year 2019 marks the twentieth anniversary of one of the deadliest school shootings in the United States. The Columbine High School massacre happened on April 20, 1999, in Jefferson County, Colorado. Two young men in their teens killed thirteen people and injured twenty-one others.

On February 14, 2018, another mass shooting occurred at Marjory Stoneman Douglas High School in Parkland, Florida. Seventeen people were killed, and seventeen more were wounded, making it one of the United States' deadliest school shootings. The suspect, nineteen-year-old former student Nikolas Cruz, was charged with both murder and attempted murder.

High school parents aren't the only ones who have to rely on faith while sending their children to school. Our nation watched in horror while the youngest school shooting victims' lives were taken in the Sandy Hook Elementary School shooting that occurred on

December 14, 2012, in Newtown, Connecticut. Twenty-year-old Adam Lanza fatally shot twenty six- and seven-year-old children, as well as six adult staff members. Before driving to the school, Lanza shot and killed his mother at their home. When first responders arrived at the school, Lanza took his own life by shooting himself in the head.

Not only has the number of school shootings continued to rise, but the number of mass shooting incidents worldwide has increased as well.[4] They have become too frequent for anyone's comfort. Comedy host Conan O'Brien was troubled by the fact that there have been so many mass shootings that his staff created a "remark" file about them. He said a writer on the show had approached him with an archive of comments he'd made on the air after prior shootings.

The *LA Times* captured his response in October 2017, after the deadly Las Vegas, Nevada, mass shooting:

> I've been doing this job for more than 24 years, and when I began in 1993, occasions like this were extremely rare. For me, or any TV comedy host back then, to come out and need to address a mass shooting spree was practically unheard of. But over the last decade, things have changed. . . . How could there be a file of mass shooting remarks for a late-night host? When did that become normal? When did this become a ritual? And what does it say about us that it has?[5]

O'Brien asked some tough yet thought-provoking questions and the subject matter is reflective and proof that we live in a world where faith is needed in our daily lives. You need faith to believe the best. Faith is simply the ability to see something you can't see with your natural eye. It is choosing to see what is still yet to come. You lift your eyes above what you see in the natural realm and focus on something that is yet to be. If you're going to go back to school to get your degree, you're going to need to have faith. You've got to see yourself walking across that stage with that graduation gown on before it happens. A faith perspective goes hand in hand with helping you hold on to your hope.

Storm Playbook Study

Chapter Summary

- Perspective unlocks multiple vantage points, which can multiply your opportunities for success.
- Even when the world seems to be falling apart, perspective is critical because a positive outlook can create a favorable outcome more quickly.
- Coping mechanisms frequently determine the difference between surviving and thriving.
- There are positive and negative coping mechanisms. It is important to learn and understand them so that you do not adopt the negative ones.
- It is important to live life realistically, with your eyesight combined with insight that is gained through revelations from God.

Journaling

1. Think about the concept that "hurting people hurt people." In what ways will you reach out to those around you who seem to be in pain?

2. What coping mechanisms from the chapter do you currently use? Which positive ones can you implement while eliminating the negative ones?

Storm Survivors: Shiphrah and Puah

As we increase our insight, our eyesight will become sharper. Meaning, we will begin to develop precise strategies and the bravery to navigate through and out of storms that may be risky but necessary. This story precisely reveals the power of insight through these two ladies.

> The king of Egypt said to the Hebrew midwives, whose names were Shiphrah and Puah, "When you are helping the Hebrew women during childbirth on the delivery stool, if you see that the baby is a boy, kill him; but if it is a girl, let her live." The midwives, however, feared God and did not do what the king of Egypt had told them to do; they let the boys live. Then the king of Egypt summoned the midwives and asked them, "Why have you done this? Why have you let the boys live?"
>
> The midwives answered Pharaoh, "Hebrew women are not like Egyptian women; they are vigorous and give birth before the midwives arrive."
>
> So God was kind to the midwives and the people increased and became even more numerous. And because the midwives feared God, he gave them families of their own. (Ex. 1:15–21)

These two brave midwives defied the king because they feared God, and God not only spared their lives but blessed them with families of their own. These women were quick on their feet and provided a suitable explanation for why the boys had lived. These women wisely feared the Lord, and as a result many lives were saved.

In a day and time where people compromise their standards and beliefs, it is important that we use our insight as well as our eyesight. Our eyesight would suggest that people are no longer following the commands of the Bible, but our insight helps us understand that God's Word is true yesterday, today, and for-evermore. He is Alpha and Omega, and His Word does not change. We serve a faithful God who still requires faithfulness from His people.

The same way these Egyptian midwives heroically saved the lives of countless helpless infants, we, too, must embrace the per-spective to fight for justice in our communities, states, regions, and countries.

Memory Verse

Therefore, since we are surrounded by such a great cloud of wit-nesses, let us throw off everything that hinders and the sin that so easily entangles. And let us run with perseverance the race marked out for us, fixing our eyes on Jesus, the pioneer and per-fecter of faith.

—Hebrews 12:1–2

CHAPTER 8

Rebuilding Season

Rebuilding is a significant endeavor because it involves a series of major activities to produce the desired result. At times the devastation that has occurred is so extreme, reconstructing the various areas will require months or even years. Rebuilding—whether in the natural realm or in life—over an extended period is considered a *rebuilding season*.

As a pastor, I teach that at some point everyone will face the need to construct or reconstruct four important areas of life. Those areas are *spiritual*, *physical*, *relational*, and *financial*.

Dealing with these areas can be tricky because they tend to affect one another. As I mentioned earlier, a bad relationship can impact your money issues, and coping with a terminal illness can take a toll on your relationships. After facing your storms, it is imperative that you focus on rebuilding in the affected area so it doesn't negatively impact other aspects of your life.

Rebuilding Spiritually

First, let's talk about rebuilding spiritually, by which I mean your inner being. Your inner being is also connected to your mind and what you think. If you're not healed in your soul, emotions, or thinking, then you're not going to experience success. Some issues are spiritual problems while other things are soul problems. If you don't get your inner being together, you're not going to experience success as you should. Your inner being is your internal reservoir of strength and peace. As Christians, we practice a lifestyle of prayer and worship to protect our hearts, which the Bible refers to as our "wellspring of life" (Prov. 4:23 WEB). Attending worship services and church events helps to refill us as believers. Some individuals do not attend church but rely on meditation to refuel. I have found that people who believe in a higher power, regardless of their belief system, generally have more peace and joy than those who don't.

If you are someone who continually feels tired, depressed, and stressed out, I suggest that you need a spiritual rebuilding season. There are many ways to do this, such as going to an inspirational conference, finding a spiritual counselor to talk to, or joining a church or another organization that can help you fellowship with others and restore your joy and peace.

A spiritual rebuilding season is especially important when dealing with storms that have left you feeling abandoned, attacked, or violated in some way. Spiritual storms are just as devastating as losing all your life's possessions to a hurricane, earthquake, or tornado. They include dealing with broken promises, experiencing acts of violence (as a witness or victim) or enduring an incident of assault or abuse (physical or sexual), drug or alcohol addiction, or failures.

A rebuilding season is necessary because these experiences affect your heart, mind, and soul; a spiritual reset is needed.

Rebuilding Physically

The next type of rebuilding season is one that requires recovery, picking up the pieces from a physical ailment or affliction of some kind. The stressors that you experience during a serious illness can take a toll on you and everyone affected. Even after you survive the diagnosis and treatment, your life is often altered severely. For some, daily tasks are now difficult or impossible; for others, diseases or accidents could have caused a permanent difficulty such as paralysis or loss of a limb, of vision, or of the ability to speak. These catastrophic storms require a rebuilding season of healing for your body and your mind. Your mind must accept your new limitations, and you must be diligent to follow the doctor's instructions. For many, this means learning a new level of discipline. For example, after a heart attack, the doctor often gives patients dietary restrictions. I have encountered many people who end up back in the hospital because they refused to change their diet. As a pastor, it saddens me when I have parishioners ask me to pray for conditions that could have been prevented through better choices. With regular visits to the doctor and more care about what we do with our bodies (both inside and outside), we can avoid many physical hardships or reduce the length of a physical rebuilding season.

I think my husband is a good example of this, so I want to give a shout-out to him. Recently he was diagnosed with both diabetes and high blood pressure, which was a surprise. At first, he didn't really want to tell me because he had always had a perfect doctor's report. However, no spouse should keep anything significant from their mate. I observed him and knew something had changed. He was taking his blood pressure every day and refusing certain foods. I finally asked him what was happening, and he mumbled through the explanation. I left him alone because I understood what was going on. He was struggling with fear. He didn't want his health to decline so much that he would end up like his mom, who had become very ill from diabetes and passed away when he was only sixteen. He finally told me the diagnosis, showed me his meds, and started working to lose weight and maintain a healthy diet. He hates defeat and is one of the most disciplined people I know; many will testify of this truth. Each day I watched him exercise for an hour and eat oatmeal, salmon, and spinach (even on vacation). At first, I thought he was being extreme, but in four to six months, he had lost thirty pounds. The doctor took him off the medication because he had reversed the diabetes. You go, honey!

Physical trauma can hit you hard and may require not a day or a week but a season of rebuilding. It will take both inner and mental strength to process what's really going on and to maintain the courageous mind-set to conquer it. I have found that inner strength produces faith, and faith can manifest what one desires and prays for.

Another thought I want to share is this: a person's successful recovery from traumatic events mainly depends on the core of that person. Now, this is not to repeat the discussion on inner strength but to dig a little deeper. I have discovered from my own struggles and from observing others that the core of a person can make or break them. Do you agree? If so, then perhaps you're like me and are asking the deeper question: Can the core of a person be changed? Core values are the fundamental beliefs of a person. These guiding principles dictate behavior and can help the person understand the difference between right and wrong. Also, core values engage one's heart and mind to define their true self.

Your core values make up your internal GPS that navigates you through all of life's hills and valleys. Core values are formed in many ways. They are the collected sum of your inherited traits, learned behaviors, and environmental factors.

However, depending on how a person's life experiences have defined those values, they can be counterproductive. Take the example of a person who has patriotism as a core value and is unexpectedly hospitalized in a foreign country. That person may reject care from the foreign hospital out of their devotion to their own country. Another example is a person who has self-reliance at their core and consistently rejects help from others. I've known people who were surprised when their loved one suddenly became very sick and passed away. They said, "We never knew. He never told us he was sick or asked for help." Or, "She used to always say, 'I never want people to worry about me.'" This is a heartbreaking experience for those who must walk through it.

A core value may never change in someone. However, I believe that circumstances can change a negative into a positive, which can shape a person's core values. I've seen it happen, especially after storms. Because storms can shake a person to their core, it can be the ideal time for something new to develop that can guide them to future victory. Many times, however, it will require interaction with others before such a change can happen.

Rebuilding Relational Ties

Rebuilding relationships in the aftermath of a storm is one area I continue to mention in this book. Why? Because they affect so many aspects of our lives.

When people are shaken by storms, they are often ready for the right person to bring about positive change in them, to help them let go of the negative impact they've experienced. This type of recovery may benefit from a God-ordained relationship in particular. I have seen so many people choose to suffer alone, but they don't have to when there are people qualified and willing to help make things better. Because of their core beliefs, some people still feel they should be able to figure out their own solutions. Either self-reliance has turned into pride or selflessness has turned into foolishness that says, "I'm not important."

Of course, there is a time and place for "alone time." Man was designed to break away from the world so that he would not break down. Genesis 2:2 says, "And on the seventh day God ended his work which he had made; and he rested on the seventh day from all his work which he had made" (KJV). I take "me time" regularly because my profession requires me to be with people constantly to help them solve problems. I love what I do, but to be effective, I must take time away from everyone to be renewed. During that time, I pray, study, and meditate on information that can help me help them.

My principles are founded on my biblical beliefs and experiences gained during my forty-one years of marriage and during the decades that I have provided pastoral counseling to couples and individuals. As I reflected on the first theme made known in the Bible, I realized it was relational. In the Scriptures, God made it clear that He did not design man to be alone or lonely:

> And the LORD God formed man of the dust of the ground, and breathed into his nostrils the breath of life; and man became a living soul. . . . And the LORD God said, It is not good that the man should be alone; I will make him an help meet for him. (Gen. 2:7, 18 KJV)

God at His core is relational, and since we are made in His image, at our core we are relational as well. He designed us to interact with people. Human beings should love, care for, and interact with other human beings. Some people love their pet(s) but not other people. Something is slightly strange about that. Our God-core should prompt us to be relational. However, God went even further and said man needed a more suitable companion for him, or a helpmeet.

God Himself desired relationship with man. He made man and breathed life into him. He named the first man Adam and gave him the ability to walk, talk, and develop what was given to him. Notice that the Bible says God made Adam a living soul, and He socialized with Adam and taught him about the environment. When animals were not adequate to fulfill Adam's needs relationally, God created woman from Adam's rib, and the woman, too, became a living soul. God refused to be alone, and He refused to leave Adam alone. All this is relational.

When situations arise that tear down our ability to be relational, then we should realize something is wrong. God always provides someone to talk to about our situations, nearby or far away—someone who has expert information or skills and who can change our core through therapy, or someone who can give companionship, friendship, prayer, and love. I believe that when God created Eve, the only other human on earth with Adam, He was sending a message not only about marital relationships but about friendship as well. Of course, we know that everyone will not get married or even wants to, but everyone can have friends.

After Katrina, many people had to rebuild their marriages as well as their houses. When trauma shakes us at the core, it can reveal that we have not been true to ourselves or to our mates.

Pressure can also bring out things about a person that were never seen before. I was saddened to see people walk away from long-time marriages after the storm. Sometimes I was able to learn the details of why they split. Most of the time it was because they had discovered that their mate, at their core, didn't have the same values that they did.

For instance, some realized that when they lost their material possessions, their mate felt as if they no longer had a marriage. While one was willing to stay and rebuild, the other felt that rebuilding with little or nothing was impossible. Others broke up because the responsibilities had shifted from two people to just the one person who was still employed after the storm. Some felt that it was not their responsibility to take care of everything alone, so they left. Others simply were too depressed to go on. Devastation had wiped out or exposed their lack of faith and confidence.

So you see, it is so important, during dating or the engagement period, to find out something about that person's core values. If you're already married, you should tenderly talk about what is important to you both and merge your values to create a solid marriage.

Core Principles of Marriage

There are some basic principles that I teach concerning marriage. When I counsel couples after storms, I sometimes notice that because they had never taken the time to set up their marriages properly, they were not able to withstand a storm's aftereffects. In response, I wrote a book titled *The Two Shall Become One*. I believe it's important to understand that whatever each of you brings into the marriage, you both will become one with it. For example, if you bring joy, you both will be joyful, but if one brings lying, both of you will become one with lying at your core. Therefore, you both must be on guard against, resist, and communicate about anything that is unhealthy, unwholesome, or unacceptable to you, because if it remains, it will grow in the marriage and become a greater issue.

Marriage is spiritual according to the Scriptures. Marriage is a result of the power of agreement. When you say "I do," you are saying you agree with this other person. However, if you don't agree, I suggest that you make it known; otherwise there will be trouble down the line. The phrase "the two shall become one" is a prophetic statement about marriage, but what "one" will the couple become? Will the woman become more like the man or the man more like the woman? God revealed years ago that it will not be either of these; instead, the couple will become a blended "one" that is presented back to God as a "new one." Unfortunately, this statement has been taken too lightly, or, in many cases, it was never taken seriously, especially in the time we live in today.

If you are someone who has experienced relationship difficulty, you need to take time to grieve the relationship you lost and then to understand why you lost it. So often we make the same relationship mistakes. Because the pain of losing a relationship is so great, we quickly enter the next one without taking the time to heal from the last relationship. My advice to you: take some time and figure out your strengths and weaknesses as well as what your ideal relationship is. Decide what your nonnegotiables are and don't compromise on those things. If your idea of a perfect date is eating at a seafood restaurant that has outdoor dining, and you meet someone who can't stand the smell of fish and hates the outdoors, then perhaps the two of you should just be friends. Unless the two of you are okay with alternating where you go and what you eat, one will end up resenting the other because they will feel forced to do something they don't like.

On the other hand, if you find someone you are compatible with and with whom you agree in most areas, it will go a long way in reaching relationship happiness. Ultimately that is what you want, because only unhealthy people get into relationships that are filled with drama, discord, dysfunction, and disagreement. And the last thing you want after taking personal time to heal from a bad relationship is to get involved in another one. Do yourself a favor and recover thoroughly from your broken heart so that you can make an excellent choice for yourself. You will be so glad you did!

Rebuilding Financial Security

For many people, a season of financial rebuilding is unavoidable after a storm. If you or anyone you know has experienced severe financial debt, bankruptcy filing, repossessions, low credit scores, tax debt, back child-support payments, or credit card debt, then you know firsthand the stress that can be caused by financial challenges.

In February 2018, I was introduced to a new term: *financial infidelity.* I read an article from NBC News about it that stated, "If you're consistently hiding money problems from your partner, there may be a power imbalance in the relationship, or you're not on the same page when it comes to finances and your goals."[1]

This statement made so much sense to me. I often meet couples who are "financial opposites." These couples are made up of two people who think about money in completely different ways. For example, the wife may spend every dollar she makes, and the husband may put all of his extra money in savings, or vice versa. Different upbringings or significantly different financial goals influence attitudes toward money.

If you are struggling in this area and you are single or divorced, I suggest you take some time and learn how money works. You can do this by reading books, finding a financial adviser, or taking a course on budgeting or finance.

If you are married, then the first step of a financial rebuilding season is communication. Most couples come from different backgrounds. Their view of many things, especially finances, can be very different. One may believe in saving for a rainy day, and the other may think they should live it up every day and let the future take care of itself. One may believe in tithing and supporting the work of the ministry, and the other may not. You need to talk about your goals, such as paying off debt, buying or refinancing major purchases such as houses or cars, planning for retirement, creating a rainy-day savings fund for unexpected expenses, or creating college savings accounts for your kids. The aforementioned is not an exhaustive list, but it will get you started.

A ship can go in only one direction at a time. The two of you should decide which way that will be. In counseling couples, I always suggest that the one who is more skillful and mature in an area should lead in that area of the marriage. Of course, that is after love and trust make up the foundation of the relationship. Beware: fear can be an enormous roadblock in this area.

In marriage, there must be a plan. This plan must be a collaborative effort. "Two shall become one" is truly a prophetic statement. And the "two" need to talk before they become "one" so that they have the chance to form the marriage of their dreams.

During and after Katrina, fear gripped many people because the storm had wiped out everything they owned in only a few days' time. They could not control the weather, but even the things they could control were not in place, such as money in the bank, insurance plans, or, for some, retirement plans. This was devastating. Fortunately for me, even before Katrina I had begun to save consistently. Post-Katrina, I was recommended to an insurance company and met with a financial adviser. Nothing is totally sure, but when you invest with a reputable company, if you become ill, unemployed, or disabled, your company will take care of most all your needs. However, securing insurance and a retirement plan, once again, requires discipline and sacrifice. Your future has to be important to you. At your core you have to care about not leaving your loved ones financially burdened. I purchased a policy that will gift each of my grandbabies a particular amount of money when I pass away. With a little preparation and a commitment to saving, it's never too late to get ahead. Here are some financial tips I learned:

- **Downsize your lifestyle.** No retirement plan can ever work if you spend everything you make. While it may seem like a sacrifice now, trimming anything out of your budget that isn't a necessity will free up money to bankroll your future.
- **Take advantage of lifetime contributions.** Are you age fifty or older? You can make catch-up contributions of up to $6,000 for 401(k)s or $1,000 for IRAs in 2017—these may provide tax-advantaged savings benefits too. Changes

can occur quickly, so please check with your financial planner or banker to discover the best option for you.

- **Ease into retirement.** Opting for part-time work instead of fully retiring allows you to earn income that you can either put away for retirement or use to lessen the need to withdraw from your retirement assets—or both.
- **Maximize your contributions.** Start socking away at least 15 percent of your gross annual salary—or more, if you can afford it.
- **Reduce debt.** Carrying debt into retirement is a retirement income killer. Make paying off large debts, such as student loans and high-interest credit cards, a top financial priority.
- **Talk to a financial adviser.** Beyond these catch-up basics, talk to your financial professional about more complex things, like how long your expected savings will last and how you can maximize your Social Security benefits.

The last thing to consider in a financial rebuilding season is adding another revenue stream. We live in a side-hustle culture. Almost everyone I know is selling something in addition to having a full-time job or profession. Creating a source of additional income can be very helpful in meeting your financial goals in a shorter period. Know that even though a financial storm can be terrible to recover from, it is possible if you take the time to rebuild correctly. Since Katrina, I now have several streams of income. Some I sought out and others came to me because of God's favor.

You may require a season of rebuilding in these four areas at some point in your life. When storms hit one or more of these areas, you will greatly benefit from taking some time to focus on rebuilding. Focusing will help you become crystal clear on your personal goals and purpose in life. Some storms come without warning, and others occur as a result of mistakes that we make when we are moving through life without intentionality. The sooner you become clear on your vison and life goals, the simpler all the other decisions will be.

It is important that you realize how valuable you are. You are one of a kind, an original creation. You matter. You are not a mistake. You were meant to be here in this period on the earth. God put effort into creating you. He put so much detail into creating you that the Bible says that He knows the number of hairs on your head. Because God took the time and effort to create you, be sure to take time to discover your calling, gifts, and talents. Once you do, put them into action!

Unfortunately, it often takes a storm to show us just how strong we are. Sometimes you discover your greatest strength in the moment of your most significant adversity. So, while you are rebuilding, take time to reflect and come to the realization of who you are. One of the challenges with the culture we live in is that many of us (especially millennials) focus on celebrities and who they are and what they stand for. Now, having a favorite celebrity is cool. I just want to make sure that you know who you are and that you are clear on your values. I often hear people discussing the relationships and lives of celebrities when their own relationships need work. It is easy to get so absorbed in others' lives that we neglect our own.

A rebuilding season is an opportunity to learn more about yourself than you may ever have wanted to know. A rebuilding season will show you who your true friends are and who your enemies are. Often we get tripped up because we don't understand the difference between the two. We live in a time of frenemies. *Merriam-Webster* defines a *frenemy* as "one who pretends to be a friend but is actually an enemy."[2] As a woman of a certain age, I was a bit confused by this term. It sounded like what my generation used to call "two-faced," which was used to describe a person who acted one way around you but another way when you were not around. As a matter of fact, the O'Jays created an entire song about this type of people titled "Back Stabbers." For those of you who aren't familiar with the song, I will share one phrase from it that makes my point: "Smiling faces sometimes tell lies."

Backstabber was a precursor to the term *frenemy*. To me, those are the worst kind of people. I like to know the type of person I am dealing with up front. Some of the worst storms of my life were those that exposed the genuine intent of a person toward me. Even in ministry I have dealt with jealousy and betrayal. I learned some valuable lessons. I gained the ability to discern the true intentions of an individual because enemies do not operate in the same way as friends do. Some enemies disguise themselves as admirers, but they are only around long enough to get what they want out of you. Other enemies are people who do not intentionally set out to hurt you but still inflict pain in their actions. Some people just don't like you, and their sole purpose is to destroy you. Once you detect and get rid of your enemies, you can then draw your friends, your real friends, close to you. Friends are crucial because they bring a much-needed benefit to a rebuilding season: accountability. Real friends will assist you with staying on track with your goals. They will let you fuss long enough to vent but not so long that you're ready to fight someone. Real friends will allow you to cry on their shoulder but will refuse to let you slip into an ongoing pity party. Real friends want the best for you and are determined to help you reach your goals. Knowing who you really are—as well as knowing those around you—is crucial in your rebuilding season.

Rebuilding seasons show us the areas in our lives that need an overhaul. Often it takes getting to the rebuilding season to reach the path of change. To activate your path to change, you must be open to instruction. Sometimes a word of wisdom from someone who has already been where you are trying to go is priceless. I know many people who have benefited from having a mentor. Ultimately a good mentor is someone who has achieved a goal that you are striving to reach and is willing to assist you along the way. After this period of discovery and finding the right people to have with you in this season, be determined to keep moving forward!

The last aspect of achieving success in a rebuilding season is the determination not to look back. In the Bible, Lot's wife looked back and was turned into a pillar of salt. Can you imagine the memes that would be created about Lot's wife if she lived today? The internet meme creators would have had a field day with her. I digress. My point is, once you survive your storm and enter your rebuilding season, you cannot afford to look back. You have no time to waste; you must keep pushing forward.

Storm Playbook Study

Chapter Summary
- There are four areas that typically will need to be rebuilt or repaired during the course of your life. Those areas are:
  - Spiritual

- ⊚ Physical
- ⊚ Relational
- ⊚ Financial
- Each area requires different strategies to overcome defeat and proclaim victory.
- Some areas may require you to seek support from outside qualified and trustworthy individuals.

Journaling

1. Out of the four areas mentioned in this chapter, which one are you struggling with the most? Why?
2. Out of the four areas, in which area are you the strongest? Would you be willing to help others who may need a trustworthy individual to assist them in obtaining success in this area?

Storm Survivor: Nehemiah

I am captivated by the heart and servant leadership of Nehemiah. When Nehemiah heard of the ruins of the walls of Jerusalem, he was grieved to the point of weeping. Not only did he lament over the issue but he was determined to fix it as well. He used all the components of this rebuilding chapter during his process.

First he addressed issues spiritually. He repented by praying and crying out to God. He reminded the Lord of both the curse and the blessing that He had previously issued to the people of Israel:

When I heard these things, I sat down and wept. For some days I mourned and fasted and prayed before the God of heaven.

Then I said: "Lord, the God of heaven, the great and awesome God, who keeps his covenant of love with those who love him and keep his commandments, let your ear be attentive and your eyes open to hear the prayer your servant is praying before you day and night for your servants, the people of Israel. I confess the sins we Israelites, including myself and my father's family, have committed against you. We have acted very wickedly toward you. We have not obeyed the commands, decrees and laws you gave your servant Moses.

"Remember the instruction you gave your servant Moses, saying, 'If you are unfaithful, I will scatter you among the nations, but if you return to me and obey my commands, then even if your exiled people are at the farthest horizon, I will gather them from there and bring them to the place I have chosen as a dwelling for my Name.'" (Neh. 1:4–9)

Next, he asked for relational favor with the king; because he was the cupbearer and the Lord honored his wishes, he did in fact find favor with the king (1:11; 2:1–9). Finally, he had to have the physical strength and the laborers, as well as the materials (which required financial provision), to complete the task he set out to do. Although he faced ridicule and opposition, ultimately the task was accomplished and the walls of Jerusalem were rebuilt.

I am praying that in your rebuilding season, favor will be granted to you in the area you need it. I ask that you do as Nehemiah did: repent and pray to God, asking Him to show you any sin in your life that could hinder your breakthrough or your blessing.

Memory Verse

Not that I have already obtained all this, or have already arrived at my goal, but I press on to take hold of that for which Christ Jesus took hold of me. Brothers and sisters, I do not consider myself yet to have taken hold of it. But one thing I do: Forgetting what is behind and straining toward what is ahead, I press on toward the goal to win the prize for which God has called me heavenward in Christ Jesus.

—Philippians 3:12–14

CHAPTER 9

The Rebuilding Process

Grab Your Gear

The rebuilding process is fraught with dangers and unexpected happenings, so it's important to protect yourself. Think of those whose occupations require protective gear, including astronauts, firefighters, and hazmat teams. They wear clothing that helps protect their bodies from physical harm. At construction sites, the workers wear hard hats to protect their heads. Linemen who work on electrical lines wear goggles, hard hats, and gloves. Imagine if there were a suit that could protect you from everything you might encounter on this journey. I think there is!

There are specific traits I encourage you to adopt that will protect you while you are under construction. It's likely that while you are rebuilding after one storm, another storm will hit. In the story of Job, God allowed Job to be tested and he faced one calamity after the other. Sometimes our lives feel like Job's, so I urge you to become "stormproof" by developing eleven protective traits.

In order to make it easy to remember, I created an acronym out of the word *stormproof* that describes these ten protective traits and a visual diagram to help you remember them.

S.T.O.R.M.P.R.O.O.F. SUIT

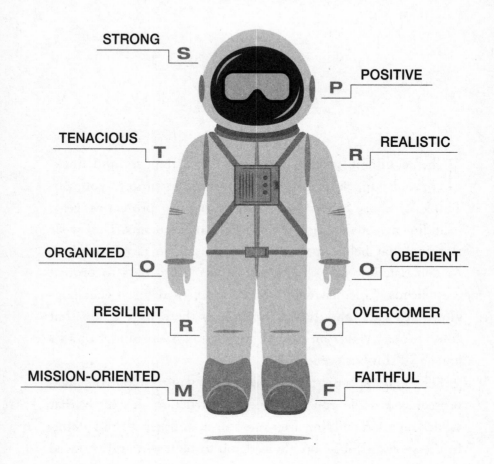

STRONG — S

POSITIVE — P

TENACIOUS — T

REALISTIC — R

ORGANIZED — O

OBEDIENT — O

RESILIENT — R

OVERCOMER — O

MISSION-ORIENTED — M

FAITHFUL — F

S—Strong

In order to protect yourself while you are in the rebuilding season, you are going to have to be and remain *strong*. If you lack strength physically or mentally, I suggest you read the book of Joshua. In chapter 1 the Lord came to him and assured him:

No one will be able to stand against you all the days of your life. As I was with Moses, so I will be with you; I will never leave you nor forsake you. Be strong and courageous, because you will lead these people to inherit the land I swore to their ancestors to give them.

Be strong and very courageous. Be careful to obey all the law my servant Moses gave you; do not turn from it to the right or to the left, that you may be successful wherever you go. Keep this Book of the Law always on your lips; meditate on it day and night, so that you may be careful to do everything written in it. Then you will be prosperous and successful. Have I not commanded you? Be strong and courageous. Do not be afraid; do not be discouraged, for the LORD your God will be with you wherever you go. (vv. 5–9)

Strength is required to defeat the enemy, who attempts to attack and distract us while we are focused on getting our lives back on track. The Word teaches us that when we are weak, we can rely on God's strength. One way that He strengthens us is through the Holy Spirit.

We need the Holy Spirit for a spirit-filled life. We cannot live according to God's will without the Holy Spirit. When we need assurance, the Holy Spirit is right beside us, bearing us up. When we need encouragement, the Holy Spirit is there to uplift us. When we need reminders of God's goodness, the Holy Spirit speaks to our hearts.

Romans 8:26 says, "So too the [Holy] Spirit comes to our aid and bears us up in our weakness; for we do not know what prayer to offer nor how to offer it worthily as we ought, but the Spirit Himself goes to meet our supplication and pleads in our behalf with unspeakable yearnings and groanings too deep for utterance" (AMPC).

The Holy Spirit makes us alive and keeps us alive. If we don't get our fill of the Holy Spirit regularly, we will live beneath the blessings God has for His children. The Holy Spirit is a tremendous gift for us. When we are in the Spirit, we can do anything God asks us to do. When filled with the Holy Ghost, we are joyful in every circumstance; the joy of the Lord becomes our strength.

T—Tenacious

Next, we must become *tenacious*. We must keep a firm grip on our faith and belief in not only God's power but also His power at work within us and through us. I once preached a message called "What Happened to My Go?" I explained to the congregation that the mind is a real battlefield. If you can grab hold of a concept in your mind, then nothing can defeat you in the natural realm. The key is to take authority through the Spirit so that you can operate victoriously on earth. When we neglect to do that, we allow the weapons of the enemy to immobilize us and stop our "go." The apostle Paul said, "We use God's mighty weapons, not worldly weapons, to knock down the strongholds of human reasoning and to destroy false arguments. We destroy every proud obstacle that keeps people from knowing God. We capture their rebellious thoughts and teach them to obey Christ" (2 Cor. 10:4–5 NLT).

It is important to recognize this so that we do not let fear and disappointment cripple us, which can happen even after a miraculous victory. The Bible gives us an example. Elijah had been fierce and tenacious with his handling of the prophets of Baal in 1 Kings 18. Not only did he disprove the god they served, but he was responsible for making sure that 450 of those false prophets were put to death. Elijah also showed God's power to the people so that they would know that He was the one true and mighty God. Strength and tenacity go together.

After such a powerful demonstration, Elijah should have been confident and excited about his victory, yet his mental fortitude was lacking. When King Ahab told his wife, Queen Jezebel, what Elijah had done, she was livid and determined to murder him. Her threat stopped Elijah in his tracks. If you continue to read the story, you'll find out Jezebel did not succeed, but Elijah's fear after performing such an impressive feat shows the need for stormproofing yourself. You can come out of one storm and go right into another. If you gird yourself properly, you will continue to get stronger in the process.

O—Organized

Next, you will be in a better place to rebuild and fortify yourself if you become *organized*. I once a read an article in the *Huffington Post* that gave twelve reasons why clutter ruins your life.[1] Clutter increases stress by overstimulating our minds, making it more difficult to wind down, which disrupts our sleep, and it provides a constant visual to-do list of things that need to be sorted, cleaned up, or thrown away in our environment. Clutter also makes our environment less healthy as the result of dust buildup, mold formation, and excessive animal dander. It can cause friction in relationships when clutter-ers and nonclutter-ers live under one roof. Whether it is between spouses or parents and children, there is a constant battle over the environment when there is no agreement regarding the standards of the home.

The A&E channel produces a show called *Hoarders* that showcases the stories of compulsive hoarders. Hoarding is actually classified as a mental disorder, and this show is a great way to experience clutter to the max. Watching just one episode will make you think carefully about the importance of organization. Finally, clutter can decrease your productivity and make you waste time. For example, have you ever been late for work, school, or church because you couldn't find your keys or wallet? It's probably not something that you would like to experience on a regular basis.

Organization helps your entire life run more smoothly and you can adjust more quickly when a challenge arises. I maintain an organized environment by having a designated space for everything. I find I have more time when I know where everything is. The more I walk in purpose, the more my responsibility increases. Consequently, I set out to discipline myself to become organized or hire someone to help me get organized, from my closet to my schedule to my paperwork (my weak area). Organizing can be overwhelming, but it must be done. Everything connects in some way. Things out of order impede progress, and that is a no-no.

R—Resilient

The next trait is one of my favorites. It's one of the personal themes of my life—*resilient*. My definition for resiliency is to be able to quickly recover and come out better on the other side. Don't get me wrong. There are many people who recover from life's intense blows, but not everyone comes out better. In fact, many come out bitter. I saw one of the best examples of this trait in the 2006 hit movie *The Pursuit of Happyness*, starring actor Will Smith as Chris Gardner.

Gardner is painting in his home when he is arrested for unpaid parking tickets. After he is released, he runs all the way from the jail to a job interview that he has been trying to get for quite some time. Even though he's wearing only a sleeveless T-shirt, jacket, and jeans, he still goes through with the interview, and because of his authenticity and honesty, he gets the job. Had he not been able to quickly recover and push past the setback of being jailed the day before his interview, he would have forfeited the interview and thus lost the opportunity that changed his life forever. I am inspired and encouraged at the grit it took for him to go into that room, shake each interviewer's hand, and honestly and comically share his story, thinking on his feet as they hurled questions his way. This is how we must endeavor to be as Christians. Sometimes it is easier to lie than tell the truth, but God's favor is on the righteous. Gardner's truth and persistence opened a door for him, just as the Lord does for His children as we walk uprightly with Him.

There are so many moments in the movie where Gardner displays resilience, such as when his wife leaves him and their young son and Gardner instantly becomes a single dad and chooses to raise his son by himself. As you are rebuilding and recovering, this is a great movie that will inspire you.

M—Mission-Oriented

Another stormproof trait is being *mission-oriented*. Becoming focused on completing the mission of your life purpose will help you avoid the distractions that could derail your destiny. Always keep in mind that you and I have an enemy, and he is real. His mission is to steal, kill, and destroy. The enemy will attack you through any vehicle he can, so you must keep your eyes on the prize. You can't look to the left or the right; you must remain focused on God's will and destiny for your life.

Remember the story of Peter walking with Jesus on the water? When His disciples were in the boat in the middle of the lake, Jesus started walking on the water, and Peter was able to walk on water with Him until he got distracted by the conditions around him:

> Then Peter got down out of the boat, walked on the water and came toward Jesus. But when he saw the wind, he was afraid and, beginning to sink, cried out, "Lord, save me!"
>
> Immediately Jesus reached out his hand and caught him. "You of little faith," he said, "why did you doubt?"
>
> And when they climbed into the boat, the wind died down. Then those who were in the boat worshiped him, saying, "Truly you are the Son of God." (Matt. 14:29–33)

As long as Peter stayed focused on Jesus, he was able to do the miraculous. It is the same with us in our everyday lives. We can do all things through God who strengthens us, and apart from Him we can do no great works. When I was young, at a certain time at night television programming would end. There would be nothing to watch. Today, though, we live in a time of 24-7 entertainment, and while there is nothing wrong with this in moderation, we must be careful that we are still doing the necessary work to keep us in line with the purpose and destiny for our lives. When you are in a rebuilding phase, being focused on the mission of your life is vital.

P—Positive

The *P* on our stormproof suit represents becoming and remaining *positive*. This is much easier said than done, but it is an essential element during a rebuilding season. Staying positive protects you from further damage. The truth is that every individual faces good days and bad days. Some Christians have been improperly taught to expect that a life of salvation is a life without trouble. A life with Christ does ensure that when you face troubles, you are never facing them alone. As a result of that truth, you can rejoice when trials come your way.

A recent article in *Time* magazine highlighted celebrities who were formerly homeless, one of whom I know personally: Tyler Perry.[2] He is a tremendous source of inspiration to my family. I was shocked to learn that he had lived in his car after using all his savings to produce his first play. Even with all that he had suffered and had to endure, he is one of the most positive people I have ever met. As a matter of fact, he has exhibited all the traits we have mentioned so far: strong, tenacious, organized, resilient, mission-oriented, and positive!

If someone who had to sleep in their car could remain positive, there is no excuse for those of us who have transportation, food, and shelter.

Some of the most humbling experiences I've ever had were on mission trips around the world where I met people who had so little yet were so happy. It is a wonderful reminder that positivity and happiness are completely the result of a mind-over-matter decision.

R—Realistic

This next trait can be a little tricky, but I have to tell you that we must be *realistic*. We live in a society that attempts to make people believe that if they work hard enough they can achieve anything, and that is simply not true. Have you ever met someone who was the star basketball player in high school who is still trying to play ball in his midfifties? Now, there is nothing wrong with exercise, but if that individual isn't in really good shape, eventually he is going to get hurt. Have you ever met a person who can't sing but is always auditioning for roles that require them to sing? Have you ever known a person who hates animals who then attempted to date and/or marry a person who has a dog or cat that they cannot live without?

Although some of those examples are kind of funny, a sadder one is a couple who gets engaged and never discusses the fact that one wants six kids and the other wants no kids at all. These situations are just not realistic. Not only will storms continue to arise in these individuals' lives, but these people could eventually become bitter, angry, jealous, or resentful toward people who do not agree with their desires. Being realistic is essential in relationships and in life. In relationships, proper expectations can make or break your love. As a matter of fact, nothing will sabotage your love life faster than unmet and unrealistic expectations. Reality and agreement go hand in hand.

You personally have to recognize your strengths in different seasons of your life. There are some gifts you have that you are only able to use for a season. Usain Bolt, one of the greatest track athletes ever, retired in 2017. There is no question that he was an awesome and record-breaking runner. The simple truth is that there are some gifts that have expiration dates and others that do not. I have read stories of doctors and professors teaching until they are in their eighties and nineties, and in our church, pastors preach well into their seventies and eighties. Yet the reality is that those pastors may have to speak sitting down, and they typically are not able to speak for as long as they could when they were younger. The point is, keeping a realistic perspective is a way to stormproof yourself and avoid setting yourself up for defeat. It is critical that you are honest with yourself.

O—Obedience

The next O in our suit is for *obedience*. Obedience is often a very unpopular word. In a time when people flee from accountability, obedience can be seen as old-fashioned to some, but not to God. The Bible provides the ultimate obedience guide as we are instructed to obey not only God but others as well. Let's take a closer look:

We are instructed to obey God.
Deuteronomy 11:1 says, "Love the LORD your God and keep his requirements, his decrees, his laws and his commands always."

So first we are commanded to love and obey God and follow His laws and commands. The only way we will know what instructions and decrees we are supposed to follow is to continue to study the Bible and listen to biblical teaching.

We are instructed to obey our parents.

Ephesians 6:1–3 reads, "Children, obey your parents in the Lord, for this is right. 'Honor your father and mother'—which is the first commandment with a promise—'so that it may go well with you and that you may enjoy long life on the earth.'" These verses are usually taught to children. The older generations recited these three verses together, I believe, because they wanted young people to understand that this commandment has an automatic reward, which is long life. To me, if your children grow up obeying you as their parent, then it is easier for them to apply obedience to the other biblical commands, and the result is a deeper relationship with God. One of the reasons that fathers everywhere are under such great demonic attack is because negative depictions or interactions with earthly fathers make it harder for people to have positive relationships with their heavenly Father. This is another reason I am so grateful for my husband. I believe that part of why my children have good relationships with God is because they had such a great earthly model of what a dad is: faithful, loving, kind, disciplining, forgiving, and always ready to be a blessing.

We should be obedient to our leaders.

Hebrews 13:17 says, "Have confidence in your leaders and submit to their authority, because they keep watch over you as those who must give an account. Do this so that their work will be a joy, not a burden, for that would be of no benefit to you."

One of the greatest challenges I face as a pastor is speaking truth only to have it fall on deaf ears. If you are in a good church with sound biblical teaching, do your best to follow the instructions of your leaders. Some of the repeated issues I see in couples' counseling sessions could have been avoided if the couple had followed the guidance of their pastors or had participated in a marriage retreat to keep their love flames ignited or reignite the ones that had gone out. We teach God's Word because it provides protection for God's people who apply it. Just like you have insurance for your car, God's Word is insurance for your life, and its benefits are so incredible. It protects you while you are living your earthly life and then rewards you with a heavenly one! Now that is a reason to rejoice—and obey.

O—Overcomer

This O is one of my favorites. You must become an *overcomer*! You can't hear me, but I am screaming this at the top of my lungs right now as I am writing it. Overcomers see situations differently than those around them. David heard the threats Goliath made and saw an opportunity when everyone else saw opposition.

> Now the Israelites had been saying, "Do you see how this man keeps coming out? He comes out to defy Israel. The king will give great wealth to the man who kills him. He will also give him his daughter in marriage and will exempt his family from taxes in Israel."
>
> David asked the men standing near him, "What will be done for the man who kills this Philistine and removes this

disgrace from Israel? Who is this uncircumcised Philistine that he should defy the armies of the living God?"

They repeated to him what they had been saying and told him, "This is what will be done for the man who kills him." (1 Sam. 17:25–27)

Now most people love a good underdog story, and David was the ultimate underdog. No one would look at David and know that he had been preparing for the fight of his life on the back side of the mountain protecting his father's sheep. But he had, and that is the same for many of you. This last storm threatened to take you out, but when you stood up and chose to become an overcomer, you received the necessary battle training to go and strike the head of the thing that has been attacking you, threatening your family, or making you doubt the call of God on your life. This last storm was just a setup for your blessing, and your decision to let it strengthen you instead of draining you was the prerequisite to your reaching the next level in God and in life.

Let's examine the text a little more. Once David was obedient and had completed his assigned task and dropped off the food for his brothers, he asked the men again (paraphrasing), "So what are the rewards for killing this disgraceful outsider?" Do you see that? David was confident and doing a little trash talking. You know how athletes try to intimidate one another on the field or court? That is what David was doing. He did not even refer to Goliath by name.

As we draw close to the end of this chapter, I encourage you to see yourself as an overcomer, just as David did. You may not be the biggest, you may not be the baddest, you may not be the most beautiful or the most handsome, but what you are is this: called by God to defeat every giant you face. God is using these stormy trials to equip you with what you need to obtain victory and receive the rewards that He has promised you.

F—Faithful

Finally, God requires us to be *faithful*. Scripture reminds us that without faith, it is impossible to please Him (Heb. 11:6). We all want God to be pleased with us. One of the most extreme examples of faithfulness I know of is the Old Testament story of Abraham offering Isaac as a sacrifice to the Lord, found in Genesis 22:1–18. God tested Abraham by instructing him to take his son Isaac to the land of Moriah and offer him as a burnt sacrifice. Incredibly, Abraham obeyed and saddled his donkey to take them to the mountain God had chosen.

> When they came to the place of which God had told him, Abraham built the altar there and laid the wood in order and bound Isaac his son and laid him on the altar, on top of the wood. Then Abraham reached out his hand and took the knife to slaughter his son. But the angel of the LORD called to him from heaven and said, "Abraham, Abraham!" And he said, "Here I am." He said, "Do not lay your hand on the boy or do anything to him, for now I know that you fear God, seeing you have not withheld your son, your only son, from me." And Abraham lifted up his eyes and looked, and behold, behind him was a ram, caught in a thicket by his horns. And Abraham went and took the ram and offered it up as a burnt offering

instead of his son. So Abraham called the name of that place, "The LORD will provide"; as it is said to this day, "On the mount of the LORD it shall be provided."

And the angel of the LORD called to Abraham a second time from heaven and said, "By myself I have sworn, declares the LORD, because you have done this and have not withheld your son, your only son, I will surely bless you, and I will surely multiply your offspring as the stars of heaven and as the sand that is on the seashore. And your offspring shall possess the gate of his enemies, and in your offspring shall all the nations of the earth be blessed, because you have obeyed my voice." (vv. 9–18 ESV)

There are so many powerful elements in this story, but one of the most powerful is that Abraham served God and obeyed Him faithfully—even when asked to do the unimaginable. Remember this is the same son that Abraham waited for, and then out of the blue, God asked him to sacrifice his child. I have two daughters, but I have only one son. And as much as I love God, I could not imagine being in Abraham's sandals and having to walk my son up that mountain.

Equally astonishing to me is the faithfulness of Isaac, who went on this journey, trusting his father and his God, although there was no substitute sacrifice in sight.

The lesson I want you to take away from the story is that God provided the sacrifice and gave them a blessing after they responded faithfully and obediently to do what He asked of them. Faithfulness is a setup for supernatural provision. Hebrews 11 is often nicknamed "The Roll Call of Faith" because it gives an impressive list of heroic figures from the

Old Testament. One of the most important messages people draw from Hebrews 11 is that many of these individuals went to heaven believing in something they did not get to see on earth; however, they never stopped believing. It is important that we develop these long-distance faith muscles because in the kingdom, legacy is the result of what is planted now and produces a harvest later.

I am seeing blessing in my children's and grandchildren's lives as a result of my and my ancestors' prayers. I steadfastly believe that my great-great-grandchildren are going to encounter a supernatural increase of faith because of the seeds I sow today. God gives us an opportunity to receive blessings or curses, but He cautions us to choose wisely because those decisions will affect the third and fourth generations. I don't know about you, but I want to leave a legacy of blessings. The way to do that is to adopt a lifestyle of faithfulness. It is the last component of your stormproof suit.

Storm Playbook Study

Chapter Summary

- When rebuilding, it is important to protect yourself from other storms that could delay or hinder your recovery season.
- One way to protect yourself and your progress is by adopting the ten traits that are identified in the S.T.O.R.M.P.R.O.O.F. acronym illustrated by the stormproof suit.
- To recap the suit elements:

S—Strong

T—Tenacious

O—Organized

R—Resilient

M—Mission-oriented

P—Positive

R—Realistic

O—Obedient

O—Overcomer

F—Faithful

Journaling

1. Out of all the suit elements, which ones do you already possess? Which ones do you need to work on applying to your life?
2. Can you think of anyone who would benefit from learning about the stormproof suit? If so, list their name(s) below and schedule a time to share it with them.

Storm Movie

The 2000 movie *The Perfect Storm* is described as a biographical dramatic disaster film.

1. After you watch it, what are two points you learned from the movie?
2. If you could change any part of the movie, what would it be and why?
3. Who was your favorite and least favorite character in the movie? Why?

Storm Survivor: The Wise Builder

One of my favorite components of the New Testament are the parables of Jesus. He had an extraordinary way of taking simple messages and making them clear and easy to apply to life. In this story there are two builders, and one is building on sand and the other on a rock foundation.

> Therefore everyone who hears these words of mine and puts them into practice is like a wise man who built his house on the rock. The rain came down, the streams rose, and the winds blew and beat against that house; yet it did not fall, because it had its foundation on the rock. But everyone who hears these words of mine and does not put them into practice is like a foolish man who built his house on sand. The rain came down, the streams rose, and the winds blew and beat against that house, and it fell with a great crash. (Matt. 7:24–27)

In Louisiana, we have a type of home that was popular when I was growing up called a shotgun house. One of the characteristics of these homes is that they are built two or three feet off the ground. You can imagine that in an area that is between one to twenty feet below sea level, it would make sense that the homes be built higher up to avoid flooding.

Remembering these homes gives me my own interpretation of the parable of the wise and foolish builders. In our area it makes sense to find out your elevation and flood zones before you build a house on a property or buy an existing house. In the same way, if you think about someone building their home on sand, it seems completely insane for a lot of reasons. First, sand is not consistent. Its texture changes depending on whether it is wet or dry. But we all know people who put their hope and trust in things or people who do not deserve their trust. The benefit to stormproofing is that it shows you how to properly assess other areas of your life.

When you are operating at a high level of strength and obedience, you will not allow yourself to be put into a situation that would make others question your integrity. Stormproofing creates the intestinal fortitude within you to make decisions and build your life on a solid foundation, which protects not only you but also those around you.

Memory Verse

(This is a little longer than the previous memory verses, but is important to learn, even if you learn it two or three verses at a time.)

Put on the whole armor of God, that you may be able to stand against the wiles of the devil. For we do not wrestle against flesh and blood, but against principalities, against powers, against the rulers of the darkness of this age, against spiritual hosts of wickedness in the heavenly places. Therefore take up the whole armor of God, that you may be able to withstand in the evil day, and having done all, to stand.

Stand therefore, having girded your waist with truth, having put on the breastplate of righteousness, and having shod your feet with the preparation of the gospel of peace; above all, taking the shield of faith with which you will be able to quench all the fiery darts of the wicked one. And take the helmet of salvation, and the sword of the Spirit, which is the word of God; praying always with all prayer and supplication in the Spirit, being watchful to this end with all perseverance and supplication for all the saints.

—Ephesians 6:11–18 NKJV

CHAPTER 10

Preparing for the Next Adversity

Strategies for Storm Survival

My hope is that this book reminds you that life keeps going even if the storms keep coming and that in it you will find strategies not only to survive but to thrive beyond the storms.

Many people were significantly affected when the levees failed and flooded our beloved city, but some reports existed beforehand that acknowledged the weaknesses in the infrastructure. Most of the citizens of New Orleans were unaware of that information, including me. Hurricane Katrina taught me the importance of keeping up with information about our state. In an article featured in *City Lab* in January 2018, I learned about government-funded climate relocation and specifically about the geography around Isle de Jean Charles, Louisiana, which is connected to the state only by a thin four-mile road that is inches above sea level and has steep drops-offs into the ocean on both sides. As the earth's climate continues to change, the residents of Isle de Jean Charles will eventually be forced to move off the island. They won't be alone, because there are up to thirteen million climate refugees in the United States. Some communities are already in the process of climate-related relocations, including Native American and Native Alaskan groups, but unfortunately there isn't any government funding or agency to help.[1]

This type of information is critical if we in my beloved home state of Louisiana are to prepare for the next potential adversity.

Knowledge is the key to being ready. Like David in the Bible, we are equipped to succeed when we use what we know. When David came down the mountain from tending sheep and heard Goliath insulting the Israelite soldiers, he decided to take action to defeat him. He had faith that God could put Goliath into his hands, but when Saul tried to give him armor and weaponry, David turned them down, saying he didn't know how to fight with that equipment. Instead, he decided to fight the battle with what he already knew: his sling and a rock. I've seen people with a lot of faith but not enough knowledge—or the desire to gain the knowledge—struggle to be successful.

In life, there will be some learning you'll have to do and some experiences you'll need to go through. Because of Hurricane Katrina, I learned that I needed to understand more about FEMA, the Federal Emergency Management Agency. I needed to be more involved in local politics so I would know which leaders to contact during a time of need for my community. I learned that ignorance is not bliss and people can actually, literally perish from lack of knowledge, just as the Bible warns.

Knowledge is powerful, but wisdom must go with it. I used to think if I ignored politics, problems would go away. My lack of knowledge back then cost me. I was like many people who take the easy route to escape their problems and those surrounding their city, state, and country. However, if we do this, we become as guilty as those who are not doing the right thing in office.

Those who answer the call to serve the public must be knowledgeable, wise, and courageous. Individual assignments are important, and selecting the best candidate for public offices is crucial. I have seen people step into positions and succeed even when they were inexperienced and unpopular because they sought

PREPARING FOR THE NEXT ADVERSITY

out the knowledge they needed. It became evident that they had followed God's calling and assignment for them. Usually they focused more on serving others than themselves, which I find heartwarming. It's how the world is supposed to be. This is often how historical change takes place. Is there something you have been called to do? I suggest you write it down. What knowledge do you need? Who can help you in this effort? Develop a plan and move forward. I believe in the saying, "If you fail to plan, you plan to fail."

Even those who aren't qualified can be successful. One example is Queen Esther in the Bible, whose Storm Survivor story we looked at in chapter 3. She was a poor orphan being raised by her cousin Mordecai. I've often imagined what that must've been like. Men are able to care for girls successfully, but sometimes they don't know those little details about what a girl wants and needs. I remember when I was in the hospital after delivering my third child. My husband was watching my other two. He was excellent at taking care of my son; although when they came to see me at the hospital, he was wearing mismatched clothes. But my poor daughter's hair had been left uncombed for several days. I was appreciative that he was brave enough to keep the children without any help, but I couldn't wait to get home.

Esther still grew up to be beautiful, and the king chose her to become his queen. Because she had lived in obedience to God, she became an important instrument of His will. Esther, through the power of prayer, fasting, a sharp mind, and good character, gained enough courage to go to the king. Using her insight and eyesight, not only did she become the queen, but she was also able to share Haman's evil plan with the king and save her nation.

You see how one woman's courage and obedience protected a

whole generation? Are you the one in this generation? It doesn't matter how small the needed change may be; if God calls you to do something, do it! The results will be impactful to those who benefit from it.

I want to share the following storm strategies taken from Esther's example and from my own life to assist you in preparing for your next adversity.

1. **Become a good decision maker.** Some of the most significant challenges we face are a result of making poor decisions, making decisions too slowly, or responding emotionally. It is imperative that you be able to assess a situation quickly and proactively when you can and then make a good decision as swiftly and wisely as possible.

2. **Bloom where you are planted.** Be determined to reach your desired goals, but while you are on your way, commit to blooming where you are planted. Be faithful to your job, ministry, or side hustle until it blossoms into what you want. Often we get into trouble and are unprepared for adversity because we have not developed the ability to be content while pushing toward the next level of achievement and victory in our lives. Comparing yourself to someone else is a recipe for disaster and will impair your ability to make the best choices and thrive in your current situation. If you're consistently frustrated with your life, take a moment to examine your social media feeds. Until you have reached more of your goals, you may have to unfollow some people who make you feel inadequate. Keep your eyes on your journey and power forward!

3. **Have a plan for the future.** You need a one-, five-,

ten-, fifteen-, twenty-year, and on plan. I suggest writing your plans in pencil as you allow God to direct your steps, but you need to have a plan in place so you know the direction in which you are going. We often get sidetracked when there is no plan in place and no goals we are working to achieve.

4. **Maintain a personal standard of integrity.** You should create a plan for success that doesn't require you to be cutthroat. You do reap what you sow. If you are negative and nasty, you will suffer. I know many people who have faced adverse situations because they were willing to do anything to get ahead. In the end, activities done in the dark always surface to the light, so do everything aboveboard.

5. **Build an inner circle of advisers you trust.** The Bible says, "In the multitude of counsellors there is safety" (Prov. 11:14 KJV). Sometimes surviving the next difficulty depends on the people you put in your life before the next storm hits. It may be too late to find a pastor, mentor, or leader in the middle of a tornado; the time to assemble people you trust is during a calm period in your life.

6. **Understand storms are inevitable.** If you accept that no matter who you are or what you achieve storms will come, then you will always be mentally prepared to survive the storm. So many people never expect a storm to darken their doorstep, and when it comes, the gravity of the situation paralyzes them. I don't want that to be the case for you. Of course, it's not necessary to walk around waiting for the other shoe to drop either. Ella Fitzgerald sang, "Into each and every life some rain has got to fall,"

but my husband sings a song, "The Sun Will Shine After While."

7. **Get prepared for life and death.** Storms taught me that you need to have life insurance and make sure that your family is taken care of in the event of a tragedy. You also need to have a will, and as your parents age, you need to know where all their pertinent documents are located. If you are the parents, as painful as it is, when you get to a certain age you need to share this information with your responsible adult children. Many family storms can be avoided when things are discussed up front. The last thing you want is to cause division among your family members because they are fighting over your possessions or struggling to figure out how they are going to afford your funeral. Be prepared for life, and help your family be prepared for your inevitable death.

8. **Make the most of the time you have here on earth.** The way to survive the storm is by cherishing the time you have left. Do not let people waste your time. I cannot stress intentionality enough. Be intentional with your time. It is a lot easier to deal with a storm when the rest of your life is running like a well-oiled machine.

———

I want you to know that you have the power in your hands. This Storm Playbook was written to give you a different perspective to power through the adversities that you will face in life. Whether it is a storm driven by a force of nature or one of the other types of storms that impact you spiritually, physically, relationally, or financially, know that you can obtain success in these areas. It may not happen overnight, but if you keep going you will achieve your desires. You can experience a life of fulfillment and joy in spite of the difficulties you have faced or are facing.

You don't have to yield to the nagging inner voices of defeat and misery; you can have unspeakable, unexplainable joy! The key to achieving joy is to focus. For me, I choose to look at *focus* as an acronym:

F—Forgive and Forget
O—Objective
C—Communicate
U—Unity
S—Service

F—Forgive and Forget

I choose to forgive myself first for mistakes that hindered my progress in life, and next I choose to forgive others for offenses that impacted me in some way. I choose forgiveness because it frees me from the weight of carrying the pain caused by others. And because I have a limited number of days on earth, I know I can get more done faster by choosing forgiveness. Jesus is the ultimate forgiver. He forgave a sinner on the cross, He forgave Peter after he denied Him three times, and He forgave those responsible for hanging Him on the cross. Not only did He forgive them, He asked God the Father to forgive them as well. Luke 23:32–34 reads:

There were also two others, criminals, led with Him to be put to death. And when they had come to the place called Calvary, there they crucified Him, and the criminals, one on the right hand and the other on the left. Then Jesus said, "Father, forgive them, for they do not know what they do." (NKJV)

If Jesus could seek forgiveness for those who were killing Him, surely we can forgive individuals who hurt our feelings. There is power in forgiveness, and it is always a process. I forgive until I forget. The apostle Paul said, "[I'm] forgetting those things which are behind . . . [and] I press toward the goal for the prize of the upward call of God in Christ Jesus" (Phil. 3:13–14 NKJV). At some point, you must reach above and beyond the storms. You must believe and know that if you are still here on earth, your purpose is waiting for you. You cannot let unforgiveness throw you off your course, because that is what unforgiveness does. It attaches itself to you and weighs you down, which prolongs the journey toward fulfilling your destiny and your purpose. Now, please know that there is a difference between forgiving a person and allowing them to remain in your life. Some individuals you have to forgive the same way fishermen "catch and release" fish. You must catch your offense and then let it go. The process is much easier said than done, but forgiveness is essential if you are going to focus on your future.

O—Objective

I understand that objectivity is a nonnegotiable if I am going to maintain my focus. Objectivity is required so that biased emotional thinking does not hinder progress in any area of my life. It is much harder to make decisions if I am looking at everything through the emotional lens of "how I feel" or "what I want" or "what I think is fair." I learned a long time ago that although life is not always fair, there is always an opportunity for increased favor, which often tips the scales of justice for my good. We must learn to be led more by the spirit than the flesh. It is essential for a well-balanced life. King Solomon, considered the wisest man to ever live, was presented with a tough case where he demonstrated unprecedented objectivity in a situation that would have baffled the most experienced judge. The story is found in 1 Kings 3:23–28:

> And the king said, "The one says, 'This is my son, who lives, and your son is the dead one'; and the other says, 'No! But your son is the dead one, and my son is the living one.'" Then the king said, "Bring me a sword." So they brought a sword before the king. And the king said, "Divide the living child in two, and give half to one, and half to the other."
>
> Then the woman whose son was living spoke to the king, for she yearned with compassion for her son; and she said, "O my lord, give her the living child, and by no means kill him!"
>
> But the other said, "Let him be neither mine nor yours, but divide him."
>
> So the king answered and said, "Give the first woman the living child, and by no means kill him; she is his mother."
>
> And all Israel heard of the judgment which the king had rendered; and they feared the king, for they saw that the wisdom of God was in him to administer justice. (NKJV)

Solomon remained calm and was able to discern the truth. Objectivity and discernment will be critical as you endeavor to focus and move beyond the storms that life will bring your way.

C—Communicate

Communication is also nonnegotiable. The ability to send and receive information is critical to success at home, work, and in life. I make communication a top priority throughout my day. There are so many ways to communicate in our modern context. You must learn which method works for you and do it. At times you may need to switch from an email to a face-to-face meeting. Whatever is required, you must commit to doing it to keep things moving. I'm involved in ministry and community work as well as leadership on an international level. I also have my pastimes like acquiring property and mentoring women and girls. All of these require organization and communication. Communication is so powerful that God decided to create multiple languages after people linked together and began to make plans without His approval.

In Genesis 11:3–9 we learn:

They said to one another, "Come, let's make bricks and fire them well." They used brick for stone and tar for mortar.

Then they said, "Come, let's build ourselves a city and a tower that reaches Heaven. Let's make ourselves famous. . ."

GOD came down to look over the city and the tower those people had built.

GOD took one look and said, "One people, one language; why, this is only a first step. No telling what they'll come up with next—they'll stop at nothing! Come, we'll go down and garble their speech so they won't understand each other." Then GOD scattered them from there all over the world. And they had to quit building the city. That's how it came to be called Babel, because there GOD turned their language into "babble." From there GOD scattered them all over the world. (THE MESSAGE)

God caused confusion because the people were pursuing an ungodly goal, but we should strive to convey our thoughts and feelings and be the best communicators we can be in our lives, families, churches, and work places.

U—Unity

I team up with others in order to maximize our joint efforts. Excellent teamwork and agreement are essential for a successful life. I thank God for those I have surrounded myself with and those who have chosen to surround me. I have found favor with a lot of influential people who in one way or another help me be productive in all that I do. I just celebrated thirty years of women's ministry and ten years as a pastor. This all happened "beyond the storm"! We honor and respect the gifts that each of us has to get the job done. Because of their insecurities and need to constantly be recognized, many people think they cannot rebuild successfully in a group, so they go solo. But no man is an island.

Jesus is a perfect example of how we can do it better together. He came here to earth with powerful gifts and abilities, yet He called twelve disciples to help Him with His assignment. Of course He had to train and teach them, but it paid off. They grew the kingdom of God. Because of their unified efforts, the broken-hearted were healed, the hungry were fed, and the captives of evil spirits and influences were set free. I have learned the lesson that we are "better together," as one of my spiritual sons says.

S—Service

I have dedicated my life to serving others. I choose to serve my family, church, and community in order to help people achieve their life goals. I hope and pray that I have served you by offering some concepts that will help you overcome any storm you face.

Storm Playbook Study

Chapter Summary
- Understand that storms are inevitable but you can become more prepared for them.
- Build an inner circle of advisers you trust. Sometimes storm survival is determined by the people you put in your life before the next storm hits.
- Be prepared for life and death. Create a will and keep important documents in a specific place. Share the location with at least two people you trust or hire in this area (such as an estate attorney).
- Time is a precious commodity. Do not let people waste it.
- Cherish the days you have on earth.

Journaling

1. In August 2018, we honored the life of our dear friend, the legendary Aretha Franklin. As you may have read, she did not leave a will for her estate. Do you have life insurance? Do you have a will? What steps can you take to ensure that your family is provided for and knows your wishes after your time on earth ends?

2. One of the areas we discussed in this chapter is focus. On a scale of 1–10, where do you rank yourself in each area?

   F—Forgive and Forget
   O—Objective
   C—Communicate
   U—Unity
   S—Service

How can you improve your score on the ones where you graded yourself lower than 7?

Storm Survivors: The Five Wise Virgins

Chapter 25 of the book of Matthew is all about being prepared.

In Matthew 25:1–13, there were ten virgins, but five were wise and five were foolish. This parable sends a message that some will miss God when He returns for us and some will be ready to go back with Him. In the story of the ten virgins, these women took their lamps to go out and meet the bridegroom. However, only five took extra oil for their lamps.

Then all the virgins woke up and trimmed their lamps. The foolish ones said to the wise, "Give us some of your oil; our lamps are going out."

"No," they replied, "there may not be enough for both us and you. Instead, go to those who sell oil and buy some for yourselves."

But while they were on their way to buy the oil, the bridegroom arrived. The virgins who were ready went in with him to the wedding banquet. And the door was shut.

Later the others also came. "Lord, Lord," they said, "open the door for us!"

But he replied, "Truly I tell you, I don't know you."

Therefore keep watch, because you do not know the day or the hour. (vv. 7–13)

This can be a sensitive passage of Scripture to discuss because it forces you to question which group you would be in if you were one of those ladies. Will you learn to be prepared, or will you procrastinate one time too many? It is a scary thought. To ensure you'll be ready at all times, learn the importance of preparation.

One of the worst things we can do is fail to prepare. If you are unprepared for a test, you might fail it. If you are unprepared for a trip, you end up spending more money because "convenience" is convenient for everything except your purse or wallet. I can prove it to you. Have you ever had to buy something in the airport that you would ordinarily buy at Walmart? Expensive, right? And this does not just happen at the airport. Have you ever noticed the price difference of food or medicine when you buy it in the hotel lobby versus the grocery store?

The sellers of these goods understand that under normal circumstances you would never pay four dollars for a snack-size bag of chips or eleven dollars for a contact lens case, but you will if you really need it.

Another parallel that Jesus was making in telling this story is that you must be prepared to go to heaven, and the key is to "stay ready," because you do not know exactly when He will return and it will be time to go.

Now that you have had some experience weathering storms, you know what to expect and can take the lessons you have learned to be prepared for future storms.

Memory Verse

But we have this treasure in jars of clay to show that this all-surpassing power is from God and not from us. We are hard pressed on every side, but not crushed; perplexed, but not in despair; persecuted, but not abandoned; struck down, but not destroyed.

—2 Corinthians 4:7–9

CHAPTER 11
Storm Support Team

Now that you have taken the time to learn and master the Storm Playbook, it is time for you to go out and share your lessons with someone who is struggling to survive their own storm season. If you are going to become an official member of the Storm Support Team, you must learn to function like a first responder.

I had the opportunity to get to know a member of a first response team in my area. She shared with me that the first week on the job, she didn't experience anything too traumatic. That week consisted of helping an elderly lady who was having chest pains and her husband, an older man who had fallen and his wife, a young mom who had gone into labor whose husband was deployed overseas, and a teenage boy who had broken his arm during a skateboarding incident while visiting his grandmother.

The young paramedic and her partner were able to help each patient. But the following week would keep her awake at night for the next few months. She and her partner had dropped off a nonemergency patient at the emergency room and were headed to lunch when they witnessed a car accident right in front of them.

One minute they were on their way to a restaurant and the next she heard the loudest crash she'd ever heard. Cars around their ambulance slammed on the brakes. People pulled their vehicles off to the side of the road and raced to help the victims of the car crash.

One victim got out of his car and walked over to check on the driver of the other vehicle, then quickly turned toward their ambulance, screaming, "The driver needs help, and the engine is smoking!"

The young lady's partner, who was a ten-year paramedic veteran, quickly radioed for help. After they received confirmation that police and firemen were en route, both paramedics assessed the scene. The driver could barely move without assistance.

After what seemed like an eternity, sirens began blaring in the distance. The bystanders slowly walked back to their cars since first responders were now on the scene. The paramedics started helping the driver who was standing on the street while the firemen engaged the Jaws of Life to rapidly, but safely, remove the injured driver from the smoking wreckage. She told me that although the entire incident was over in about twenty minutes, it seemed like a lifetime to her as a newbie on the first responder team.

Notice that the first responders didn't see the scene the way everyone else did. While everyone else sees the crisis of the moment, the first responder must see the situation through the lens of what actions need to be taken to fix or avert the crisis in progress. Unlike bystanders, first responders can't react emotionally to what they see. They have to respond to what they know already, and they have to react instinctively. Lives are at risk if they are unable to act correctly and quickly.

First responders must focus on the pain, wounds, and injuries at the scene but still be gentle and mindful of the people who are experiencing them. If they focus only on the injuries, then they treat the pain but ignore the person in distress. They have to be able to attend to both.

In the same way, once you have survived the storm and have been initiated through "storm survival training," you are qualified to help others and function as a "storm first responder" and provide "storm support."

You cannot judge the person who is fighting to survive their storm. Judgment prevents people from surviving and thriving beyond the storm's aftermath.

The Prodigal Son

To talk about how we should respond to someone in a storm, let's look at a Bible story favorite, the prodigal son in Luke 15.

There was a wealthy man who had two sons. The father had promised to share his wealth with them when they came of age. But the younger son wanted to experience life, so he asked his father for his inheritance early and went to a far country, away from his father. He partied until he had spent all he had and then was forced to get a job taking care of pigs. He became so hungry and desperate that he wanted to eat the pigs' food, but then he came to himself. He thought, *My father's servants eat better and live a better life than this. I'm going home.*

> But while he was still a long way off, his father saw him and was filled with compassion for him; he ran to his son, threw his arms around him and kissed him.
>
> The son said to him, "Father, I have sinned against heaven and against you. I am no longer worthy to be called your son."
>
> But the father said to his servants, "Quick! Bring the best robe and put it on him. Put a ring on his finger and sandals

on his feet. Bring the fattened calf and kill it. Let's have a feast and celebrate. For this son of mine was dead and is alive again; he was lost and is found." So they began to celebrate.

Meanwhile, the older son was in the field. When he came near the house, he heard music and dancing. So he called one of the servants and asked him what was going on. "Your brother has come," he replied, "and your father has killed the fattened calf because he has him back safe and sound."

The older brother became angry and refused to go in. So his father went out and pleaded with him. But he answered his father, "Look! All these years I've been slaving for you and never disobeyed your orders. Yet you never gave me even a young goat so I could celebrate with my friends. But when this son of yours who has squandered your property with prostitutes comes home, you kill the fattened calf for him!"

"My son," the father said, "you are always with me, and everything I have is yours. But we had to celebrate and be glad, because this brother of yours was dead and is alive again; he was lost and is found." (vv. 20–31)

What a beautiful story.

When storms, crises, or tragedies occur, there will be a victim(s). If there were no victim, there would be no need for a responder. Victims comes in all shapes, sizes, and personalities, and from all types of circumstances. Here, the prodigal son . . .

1. Made a bad decision. Sometimes people are victims of circumstances. It wasn't their fault, and we must show compassion. Other times, like with the prodigal son, things would have been different if a different decision had been made. However, haven't we all made bad decisions? Of course we have. So we must also show them grace as we have received grace. "As every man hath received the gift, even so minister the same one to another, as good stewards of the manifold grace of God" (1 Peter 4:10 KJV).

2. Had nothing left. When we come to offer help to the victims or survivors, we must come with supplies. We may not have everything they need, but whatever we have we should be willing to share. The prodigal son was going to resort to eating pig husks. No one would give him anything, but God gave him the mind shift to go back home. We must pray for mind shifts so people can move on and do better.

3. Was sad and hurting. The prodigal son in the text sounds sad and depressed. All types of emotions, stress, mental illness, and other sicknesses can come after tragedy. We must respond with love and compassion. Lyrics from an old song are still true: "What the world needs now is love sweet love." As believers, if we don't have money or food to give, we can give love, an encouraging word, a scripture, a prayer, a hug, a listening ear, or a simple conversation.

4. Still had a heart. Although he was the cause of his own dilemma, he had a heart of repentance and humility. His heart was right. We have to discern a prodigal's heart. Many times they want to do the right thing, but their faith is weak. As believers, we must try to give them hope.

The Older Brother

There are two types of responders. Some responders act like the prodigal's older brother, whose responses are found in verses 28–30.

1. The brother responded with anger (v. 28). When people in your life face storms because of their foolishness, you should not stay upset with them. Often their misjudgments have caused them to suffer already. If they learn the lesson from their challenge and don't repeat it, then you should indeed rejoice.

2. The brother responded with jealousy (v. 29). When something good happens to someone who has faced a challenge that their own bad decisions caused, don't complain about how you deserve the blessing more than they do. There are blessings you receive by just obeying God's commandments, your parents' rules, and the laws of the land. Know that your time of blessing will come, and often your reward is much sweeter because you are not receiving the consequences of the other end of a crisis.

3. The brother responded by rehashing his younger brother's faults (v. 30). There is no reason to throw other people's faults in their faces continually. They know what they did, and so does God. No person will escape the law of sowing and reaping, so the individual has a hard enough road ahead of them without you continually reminding them of their transgressions.

To Help Others Survive, Be Like the Father

As a first responder who is helping others survive storm seasons, you must be diligent to respond like the prodigal son's father:

1. The father reacted instantly, without delay (v. 22). The father responded by giving his son what he needed versus what he deserved, and the father instructed the others around him to move quickly as well.

2. The father restored the prodigal son by giving him items that would prove to others that the son still belonged to a family who loved him (v. 22). The father had the servants place a ring on his son's finger, a robe on his shoulders, and sandals on his feet. The father refused to let the son stay in the condition that he had returned in. Instead, he restored him as if he had never left. Often people need to feel our love and care rather than our punishment and unforgiveness.

3. The father decided to have a party and celebrate his son's return (v. 23). Many times people fall into trouble and then face only condemnation upon their return, which makes it that much more difficult for them to be open with others and allow themselves to receive the assistance they often need. When people are celebrated and shown unconditional love in the midst of their failing, they usually recover much faster.

The father responded just as the first responders had. He saw the wreck that was his son's life up close and personal. He surveyed the damage. He called in reinforcements from his staff to give his son immediate assistance and meet his basic needs, and then once the son was all cleaned up from his crisis, they celebrated.

Lessons Learned in the Storm

Now, there are people who repeatedly make bad decisions and require tough love, but that isn't what occurred in this story. The prodigal son made a bad decision that led to him scraping the bottom of the barrel. He learned important lessons—ones you can teach to the prodigal storm survivors in your life. Treat them with the love of the father rather than the contempt of the brother.

Those lessons include:

1. Relationships are more important than material possessions. The truth is that the prodigal son got in trouble because he wanted his father's inheritance. Instead, he could have treasured the gem of a father he had and established a relationship with him, learning everything from him that he could.

Some of the prodigal storm survivors in our lives get in trouble because they are unable to prioritize relationships and learn from people who are older and wiser.

2. Life is not a big party. The prodigal son sold his inheritance for cheap and began to party hard. Unfortunately, in the twenty-first century, some hold the misconception that life is meant to be one big party. The challenge with this is that excessive partying and riotous living are often associated with addiction. According to the Addiction Center:

- Addiction is more common than many realize.
- There were approximately 20.6 million people in the United States over the age of 12 suffering from an addiction in 2011.
- More than 20 million Americans over the age of 12 have an addiction (excluding tobacco).
- 100 people die every day from drug overdoses. This rate has tripled in the past 20 years.
- More than 5 million emergency room visits in 2011 were drug related.
- 2.6 million people with addictions have a dependence on both alcohol and illicit drugs.

- 9.4 million people in 2011 reported driving under the influence of illicit drugs.
- 6.8 million people with an addiction have a mental illness.
- Rates of illicit drug use are highest among those aged 18 to 25.
- Over 90 percent of those suffering from addiction began drinking, smoking, or using illicit drugs before the age of 18.
- Alcoholism is another form of addiction:
  - Binge drinking is more common in men; 9.1 percent of men 12 and older reported heavy drinking 5 or more days in a month, while 2.6 percent of women reported this.
  - More than 11 percent of Americans have driven under the influence.
  - Out of 16.6 million people with alcoholism, 2.6 million were also dependent on an illicit substance.
  - More people receive treatment for alcohol than any other substance.

Now, I believe in celebrations, and I love a good party, but it is essential to do all things in moderation. When excessive partying becomes part of an individual's daily life, they are often inviting storms to come in and destroy it. The storm winds are accompanied not only by addictions to drugs and alcohol but also by sex and acquaintances who act like they are friends until the money runs out.

3. The money runs out, and hard times will come. In the prodigal son's story, we learn that the son was living like a high roller until a famine hit the land. This is an important lesson, especially for young people or for people who make money quickly. Blessings are not going to shower forever; it is critical to save for a season of drought.

4. If you don't have the right circle, you will end up alone. The prodigal son came to his senses while he was alone in a pigpen. All the friends he had made while he was a big spender were gone. Choosing good friends and having people in your life to whom you can be accountable and who you can count on is significant, especially when storms come.

5. Sometimes you have to start over. The prodigal son had an earth-shattering revelation while he stood in the pig trough: his father's servants had more than he had in his current state. He realized it would be better for him to humble himself and be a servant than to subject himself to the plight of the hogs. Starting over is a very humbling lesson.

6. The storm meant to kill you can give you new life or a new perspective. When you are helping a storm survivor, it is imperative for you to help them focus on the positive aspect of the situation. After Hurricane Katrina, we ended up with churches in both Louisiana and Georgia. The truth is, we may have never had the Georgia church without the storm. Sometimes the storm puts you on the path to "new."

7. Last, the storm is an opportunity to build better, stronger, and faster. There are so many superheroes in our contemporary culture today that I can barely keep up with them all. Yet I recall back in the day there was a TV show called *The Six Million Dollar Man*. The main character of the show is the handsome and athletic Steve Austin. An astronaut, Austin becomes gravely injured during a spaceship accident. He then is rushed into emergency surgery, where a high-tech government-sanctioned process rebuilds or replaces several of the astronaut's body parts with machine parts, making him like a cyborg. When Austin recovers, his body's new additions give him the abilities of superhuman strength, speed, and other powers. Austin then puts these powers to work for good, fighting evil for the benefit of all.

The prodigal son's father treated his son the same way our heavenly Father responds to us: He puts our lives back together better, stronger, and faster. It doesn't happen without our help because faith without works is dead. But if we are willing to change and learn from the error of our ways, a better life is waiting for us on the other side of the storm.

How to Rebuild

There are a few ways that God rebuilds individuals. First, we must embrace the following principles:

1. We must look for revelation and admit to personal shortcomings. Nothing significant changes in our lives until we decide that we need to change. I have a friend who taught her daughters when they were young that "sorry means you don't do it again." I love this concept because she wanted them to understand early on that *sorry* was an action word. It was not something that was said to appease the injured party. It was a statement of fact to be issued as a remorseful apology that would be accompanied by a corresponding action.

2. We must readjust our emotional inner alarm system. When something bothers you at your core, you have no choice but to change it. When you genuinely desire to improve, your concern and passion will keep you up at night. You will monitor yourself and your reactions until you deal with the situation that misaligned your emotional center. You will change or respond in the way that is most beneficial.

I know a wife who always complained about her husband and how much *he* needed to change. One day her best friend gave her a copy of Stormie Omartian's book *The Power of a Praying Wife*, released originally in 1997. Although this book is more than twenty years old, it helped reset the complaining wife's internal emotional alarms because the first part of the book admonishes the praying wife that she must change first before expecting any significant change in her husband. Little by little, the wife began to put the prayers and activities of the book in motion, and her marriage transformed right in front of her eyes.

I know another wife who was devastated because her husband refused to go back to church. The husband and wife had worked faithfully at their church but were laid off so the church could purchase a state-of-the-art light and sound system with HD cameras. The wife quickly forgave the pastors and staff who had asked the couple to sacrifice their jobs for what was considered by the church leadership to be "the greater good." But the husband began looking into other religions and even started studying Islam. His "church hurt" had impacted his ability to believe in God. The wife did not rebuke him. She just prayed for him and asked him to attend church with her every once in a while. For more than two years, he would decline her request, even though he never stopped her or their children from attending a new church. Each morning before they left, she would make sure all of her husband's needs were met so he would not have any reason to resent her attending church.

Then, one day in the second year, when she asked him to come with her, he said yes. Today, though he is not a member, he has resumed his status as a Christian, and he regularly attends church with his family. Although the storm of "church hurt" hit their lives, the wife was determined not to act emotionally. She adjusted her emotional center to respond in a way that would be beneficial to her husband and her children.

3. **Finally, we must submit to God's timing.** Patience is a virtue, and waiting is a lost art. We usually want situations to be resolved in a "microwave minute" instead of a few "Crock-Pot hours." But the truth of the matter is some processes take longer than others. There is a big difference in having to wait to move into a house that is being built from the ground up rather than immediately moving into a house that is already constructed. From a commercial real estate perspective, there is a big difference between occupying a space that is move-in ready versus one that is built-to-suit. The commercial space that is built-to-suit requires a contractor, permits, supplies, and paint before it is ready for the business to arrange plants, wall decor, and office furniture.

Sometimes storms require the storm survivor to go through a process, and as a member of the Storm Support Team, you are well equipped to help the survivors navigate the process.

More Storms

For more than thirty years, I have been blessed to empower women through various ministries. However, the February before Hurricane Katrina hit, I felt God calling me to end the Women of

Excellence (WOE) conferences I had led for fifteen years. No one could believe it, but I was obeying the Spirit within.

My theme at these conferences was "Oh, for Grace," and I gave out five rocks in little silk bags to all the women. I told them that David had killed his Goliath with rocks, so these rocks were theirs to kill the Goliaths in their lives.

Many women protested or wept over the ending of the WOE conferences, but I was adamant about following what I felt was the leading of the Holy Spirit. It was as if we were entering a new season, and we were. Then, six months later, Katrina hit, and things were never the same.

Some women said to me, "Wow, you are spiritual; you really did hear from God." Our conference site (our church) was destroyed, New Orleans was in shambles, and the WOE leader (me) was displaced. Yes, God knew.

One year later, I started a ministry called Power Woman, which trains and empowers other leaders. My first conference was in Georgia at Chateau Elan. It was small and intimate but powerful, with women from my ministries in New Orleans also in attendance. At the beginning of the conference, we got the news that Hurricane Gustav was coming, which particularly worried those who had lived through Katrina. I pleaded with those women not to return and to stay where it was safe, but they panicked and left for their homes. I was worried but prayed. I felt it was a trick to make them miss the new thing God was doing.

Hurricane Gustav ended up being the most destructive hurricane of the 2008 hurricane season. It made landfall near Cocodrie, Louisiana, the morning of September 1 and caused serious damage and casualties in Haiti, the Dominican Republic, Cuba, and even the United States. According to The Balance, the damages were about $8 billion.[1] When I heard this report, it confirmed my feelings. I knew the enemy had used one of his biggest deterrents: *fear.* He abated their faith to steal a portion of their destiny. Of course, I understood that the women who had left the conference were concerned about their loved ones and possessions they had left behind, but I cannot stress enough that after the survival of one storm, we must increase our faith or the enemy will keep us running forever.

Can you believe there were even more storms in my life than I have mentioned in this book? Katrina is not the worst storm I've been through. I am amazed at how God has brought me through many years of storms such as the passing of my granddaughter, Katrina, Gustav, a dangerous pregnancy, and my husband's bout with cancer. These were great tests of my faith but my husband's mental breakdown was definitely one of the most challenging. The winds were blowing profusely in my life at that time. I did not go into detail about it in this book because I believe it warrants its own discussion. However, I think it will benefit you to know the great storm lessons I learned in that situation that prepared me to handle future storms. When it happened, the first thought that came to me was, *What do you do when your covering can no longer cover you?* Secondly, I was aware that there was much at stake—marriage, family, and ministry. Thirdly, we were in the fight of our lives and I was leading the battle. For sure, it was a category 5 but God saw us through. Perhaps I will share the story at later time, ordained by God.

———

Five years after Katrina, I was led to host the conference again. It was a reunion, and we had such a great time telling our survivor stories. We were different: new houses, cars, and homes, some living in different cities and leading different lives. Life is never the same after a storm.

We all will go through storms, weather storms or "whether" storms, meaning whether we are trying to do everything right or making blunder after blunder, every season is not your season for a storm. It is important, at the first hearing of its possibility, to begin to pray and rebuke any evil that can come or ask God to minimize or cancel it. Then you will know if it is necessary, that is, if it is meant to teach you "new storm lessons." Just pick up your storm book, and take your steps forward not just to survive but to *thrive*. Remember, all storms aren't bad . . . just get beyond the storm!

Storm Playbook Study

Chapter Summary
- After becoming a graduate of storm studies, you are ready to help others endure and master their storms.
- One way to assist others is to consider yourself a first responder or emergency rescue team member.
- First responders are able to both provide assistance to those suffering injuries and still be mindful of the emotional and physical pain the individuals may be experiencing.
- Never forget that while it can be easier to deal with storms that come with warnings and predictions, some storms will come with very little notice.

Journaling

1. Reflect on a time in your life where you had a person help you get through a particularly difficult storm. How did they help you specifically? How can you pass the gesture on and assist others?
2. What is the greatest difficulty you face when attempting to help someone in pain or despair?

Storm Survivor: Jonah

There are so many elements of the story of Jonah that resemble the characters in the parable of the prodigal son. First, Jonah did not want to go:

> The word of the LORD came to Jonah son of Amittai: "Go to the great city of Nineveh and preach against it, because its wickedness has come up before me."
>
> But Jonah ran away from the LORD and headed for Tarshish. He went down to Joppa, where he found a ship bound for that port. After paying the fare, he went aboard and sailed for Tarshish to flee from the LORD. (Jonah 1:1–3)

Not only did Jonah not want to do what the Lord asked him to do, but he ran away, as if he could escape the almighty God.

Next, Jonah's disobedience threatened the lives of others and got him tossed overboard. After he had been thrown into the sea, God sent a huge fish to swallow him up: "Now the LORD provided a huge fish to swallow Jonah, and Jonah was in the belly of the fish three days and three nights" (v. 17).

Jonah prayed for nine verses in chapter 2, and after three

days and nights God commanded the fish to release him. Jonah obeyed God, went to Ninevah, and told the people to turn back to God. In a similar way, the prodigal son had a revelation after finding himself eating the same food as the pigs. The prodigal son went home and was forgiven by his father, and the Ninevites repented of their sins after hearing Jonah's warning from the Lord and God forgave them. Jonah was angry that the Lord forgave them, and the elder brother was angry that the prodigal son was greeted with open arms and received special treatment from their father.

The most significant takeaway is that none of us has the right to judge others. We should aim to forgive as quickly as we want God to forgive us, and further, we should rejoice as the angels do in heaven when one soul gives their life to Christ.

Now more than ever, people need to feel and experience the love and compassion of God and His people. We cannot reach a world that will have nothing to do with us, and they will know us and want to be in community with us by our love. The greatest commandment is that we love God with all our hearts, minds, and souls, and the second is that we love our neighbors the way we love ourselves (Matt. 22:37–39). Helping people weather the storms of life is one of the most loving, compassionate, and godly things we could ever do as believers.

Memory Verse

Love is patient, love is kind. It does not envy, it does not boast, it is not proud. It does not dishonor others, it is not self-seeking, it is not easily angered, it keeps no record of wrongs. Love does not delight in evil but rejoices with the truth. It always protects, always trusts, always hopes, always perseveres. Love never fails.

—1 Corinthians 13:4–8

Acknowledgments

I'm still amazed at how our "footsteps are ordered by God." Following His lead, after several devastating and tragic events, I have been able to write this book to help others tunnel through their storms. However, it goes without saying that I did not survive or thrive after my storms without supportive and invaluable people in my life.

Thanks to my husband, Bishop Paul S. Morton, for more than forty years of love, support, and unusual trust and confidence in me. As my husband and spiritual leader, you have helped to develop me into a true woman of faith. I'm glad we were able to weather the storms together.

To my beautiful three children, Jasmine, PJ, and Xani, you are my greatest accomplishments. Both you and your children are my joyful reasons for living.

To my greater church family, thank you for loving and supporting me on this journey. There has been no greater assignment or accomplishment than to serve as your pastor for the last ten years. Since I was six years old, you've been my spiritual family. We are family forever.

To my, Changing a Generation family, just as out of the dirt God formed man, out of Storm Katrina, God formed you. As I always say, "All Storms Aren't Bad." I love you and am grateful for your support and confidence in my ministry as well.

Thanks to all those who personally assist me, you know who you are! Your genuine love is evident and the feeling is mutual. Finally, to my F.G.B.C.F. family, thanks for your continuous support and prayers.

Notes

Chapter 1: Life Before the Storm

1. Barbara McCarragher, "New Orleans Hurricane History," http://web.mit.edu/12.000/www/m2010/teams/neworleans1/hurricane%20history.htm.

Chapter 2: Life Interrupted

1. Kim Ann Zimmermann, "Hurricane Katrina: Facts, Damage & Aftermath," Live Science, August 27, 2015, https://www.livescience.com/22522-hurricane-katrina-facts.html.
2. Zimmermann, "Hurricane Katrina: Facts, Damage & Aftermath."
3. Zimmermann, "Hurricane Katrina: Facts, Damage & Aftermath."
4. Justin Nobel, "A Katrina Relocation Project So Ambitious It Was Doomed to Fail," *Newsweek*, August 15, 2015, https://www.newsweek.com/2015/08/28/katrina-anniversary-michael-thomas-canadaville-363131.html.
5. Todd Leopold, "Return to the 'City That Care Forgot,'" CNN, August 12, 2015, https://www.cnn.com/2015/08/12/opinions/new-orleans-katrina-city-care-forgot/index.html.
6. Benedict Carey, "Life After the Storm: Children Who Survived Katrina Offer Lessons," *New York Times*, September 8, 2017, https://www.nytimes.com/2017/09/08/health/katrina-harvey-children.html.
7. Rick Jervis, "Katrina Q&A: New Orleans Before and After the

Historic Storm," *USA Today*, August 27, 2015, https://www
.usatoday.com/story/news/2015/08/27/katrina-new-orleans
-hurricane-louisiana/32431935/.

8. Zimmermann, "Hurricane Katrina: Facts, Damage & Aftermath."
9. Hayden Packwood, "Crock-Pot Under Fire After Heartbreaking
'This Is Us' Episode," WGRZ News, January 26, 2018, https:
//www.wgrz.com/article/news/entertainment-news/crock-pot-under
-fire-after-heartbreaking-this-is-us-episode/75-511786778.
10. Caitlin Miller, "What Does Hurricane Category 1, 2, 3 . . .
Really Mean?" *Coastal Living*, accessed September 13, 2018, https:
//www.coastalliving.com/lifestyle/whats-the-difference
-hurricane-categories.
11. Matt. 19:5.

Chapter 3: Maturity

1. Katie Lobosco, "Student Loan Debt Just Hit $1.5 Trillion. Women
Hold Most of It," *CNN Money*, June 5, 2018, https://money.cnn
.com/2018/06/05/pf/college/student-loan-stats/index.html.
2. John C. Maxwell, *The 17 Indisputable Laws of Teamwork*
(Nashville: Thomas Nelson, 2003).
3. Nilofer Merchant, "Got a Meeting? Take a Walk," TED, February
2013, https://www.ted.com/talks/nilofer_merchant_got_a
_meeting_take_a_walk?language=en.

Chapter 6: Holding On to Hope

1. Joseph Benson, *Commentary of the Old and New Testaments*
(1857), commentary on Proverbs 13:12, StudyLight, https://www
.studylight.org/commentaries/rbc/proverbs-13.html.
2. Bible Study Tools, s.v. "elpis," https://www.biblestudytools.com
/lexicons/greek/nas/elpis.html.
3. Marcel Schwantes, "Warren Buffett Says This 1 Simple Habit
Separates Successful People from Everyone Else," *Inc.*, January 18,
2018, https://www.inc.com/marcel-schwantes/warren-buffett
-says-this-is-1-simple-habit-that-separates-successful-people-from
-everyone-else.html.

Chapter 7: Insight Beyond Eyesight

1. Shawn Achor, *Before Happiness: The 5 Hidden Keys to Achieving Success, Spreading Happiness, and Sustaining Positive Change* (New York: Crown Business, 2013), 39–40.

2. ICIC CEO Series, "Badass Your Brand" webinar, http://icic.org /wp-content/uploads/2018/02/2018-02-20-14.59-Badass-Your -Brand.mp4.

3. Pia Silva, *Badass Your Brand: The Impatient Entrepreneur's Guide to Turning Expertise into Profit* (Brooklyn, NY: Worstofall Design, 2017), 132–35.

4. "Sorry, Despite Gun-Control Advocates' Claims, U.S. Isn't the Worst Country for Mass Shootings," *Investor's Business Daily*, February 20, 2018, https://www.investors.com/politics/editorials /sorry-despite-gun-control-advocates-claims-u-s-isnt-the-worst -country-for-mass-shootings/.

5. Lorraine Ali, "Stephen Colbert, Jimmy Kimmel and Now Robin Thede. Late-Night Hosts Who Speak to Us—and for Us," *Los Angeles Times*, October 20, 2017, http://www.latimes.com /entertainment/tv/la-ca-st-the-rundown-robin-thede-review -20171020jon-stewart-20171020-story.html.

Chapter 8: Rebuilding Season

1. Jean Chatzky, "Financial Infidelity: Why Lying About Money Can Ruin Your Relationship," NBC News, February 17, 2018, https: //www.nbcnews.com/better/business/financial-infidelity-how-lying -about-money-can-ruin-your-relationship-ncna848576.

2. *Merriam-Webster Dictionary*, s.v. "frenemy," accessed September 14, 2018, https://www.merriam-webster.com/dictionary/frenemy.

Chapter 9: The Rebuilding Process

1. MakeSpace, "12 Surprising Ways Clutter Is Ruining Your Life [Infographic]," *HuffPost*, May 12, 2017, https://www .huffingtonpost.com/entry/12-surprising-ways-clutter-is-ruining -your-life-infographic_us_59160aace4b02d6199b2eee5.

2. Sophia Morris, "Stars Who Were Once Homeless," *Time*, July 11,

2013, http://newsfeed.time.com/2013/07/11/stars-who-were
-once-homeless/slide/tyler-perry/.

Chapter 10: Preparing for the Next Adversity

1. Michael Isaac Stein, "How to Save a Town from Rising Waters,"
Citylab, January 24, 2018, https://www.citylab.com
/environment/2018/01/how-to-save-a-town-from-rising-waters
/547646/.

Chapter 11: Storm Support Team

1. Kimberly Amadeo, "Hurricane Gustav Facts, Damage and Costs,"
The Balance, April 24, 2018, https://www.thebalance.com
/how-did-hurricane-gustav-affect-the-u-s-economy-3306021.

About the Author

New Orleans native Debra B. Morton is a leader, teacher, pastor, and entrepreneur who serves alongside her husband, Bishop Paul S. Morton Sr., at Greater St. Stephen Full Gospel Baptist Church in New Orleans, Louisiana, and is the co-pastor of Changing a Generation Full Gospel Baptist Church in Atlanta, Georgia. When she was ordained as an elder in 1993, she earned the groundbreaking distinction as one of the first ordained female elders to preach in a Baptist pulpit. A Stellar Award nominee and James Cleveland award winner, she has gone on to executively produce an album and write several songs, open a home for troubled teen girls, and help her husband to rebuild and expand a great ministry. But of all her many accomplishments, she takes her greatest pride in her personal relationship with Jesus Christ and her roles as a wife, mother of three children, and grandmother of seven.